RESURRECTION

Volume 2 of
UNIVERSAL MAN

by
Florence De Groat

Devorss & Company
Box 550
Marina del Rey, California 90291

11/93

ISBN: 0-87516-456-0

Library of Congress Card Catalog Number: 81-67782

Printed in the United States of America
by Book Graphics, Inc., California

DEDICATION

to

The Lord Christ Immanuel,

> *Emmet Fox*
> *Jack*
> *Venice*
> *Annea*
> *Elizabeth*
> *Cynthia*
> *Marjorie*

and many others who have helped mightily in my own

Resurrection,

F. D. G

Contents

Part III

RESURRECTION

Part I

The Historical Fact

The Resurrection is the great Evolutionary Fact.

It is taking place in all corners of the world today. This accounts for global and Individual crucifixions and confrontations of monumental character. No crucifixion; no Resurrection. For part Truths which were held in rigid sanctity in previous ages must resolve themselves into Cosmic Truths today—or else.

The world subconscious is being cleansed. So is the subconscious of every person who chooses to move *upwards* into Christ Consciousness rather than to give up the Evolutionary Game at this crucial juncture and to slide back to the beginning of particularized manifestation. This would probably mean for him or her starting again at scratch with another Life-Wave to develop the qualities which, thru aeons of time, would bring him to another such Opportunity as we have today.

Due to the monumental work which the Lord Christ Immanuel did for us in Galilee; and particularly to the great Sacrifice when He laid down His Lordship and descended into the darkest layer of human consciousness (called "death"), the Seed was planted which is reversing the Race currents of greed, malice, and personal self-will, so that the Spark of Christ Identity which lives in each human Individual may now rise to the surface *if It will.*

Does it seem that these primitive Race currents are still rampant in the world today? This is only the boiling up from the deeps of our subconscious of the primal urges which were our only awareness of life before our Christ Identity began to be realized.

Since Galilee, every Individual in the Life-Wave has *had the chance* to receive the Message of his-her relationship to God (as a Son-Daughter of the Most High) and of his-her ability to manifest this by ensouling and embodying the Presence of the great Lord Christ Who gave His Blood (His Consciousness) that we might know our own Be-ing and be free.

Many people believe that the Lord Christ Immanuel (known in Galilee as Jesus the Christ) will shortly "come" and "rule," thus doing our Inner work for us and eliminating "the bad ones" so that we may pass comfortably into our own Christ Consciousness. The Inner Instructions which the writer has so far received concerning this are as follows.

For us, and for many others, Christ is *here*. The Inner Companionship with Him has become so real, so powerful, and so intimate, that it forms the core of the life of anyone who wishes it to be so. We know however that the degree of intimacy and completeness of this Presence depends entirely upon *our* supplying the *mental equivalent* to His Consciousness, which is the Consciousness of the Generic Man Perfected. The Generic Man includes the Individuality of each Regenerated Person; and this Individuality is enhanced rather than submerged by unifying It with the Lord Christ Immanuel.

Concerning the many present reports of Christly participation in three dimensions at this time to help us, we submit the following considerations.

1. Our own Instructions are to continue as we are, following our own *Inner* Contact until further notice, tho cooperating with *all* Good Forces.

2. "There shall be many false Christs and false prophets. By their *fruits* you shall know them."

3. The term "Christ" we are told is used by very advanced Souls as a *title* and does not necessarily refer Individually to the Lord Christ Immanuel.

4. When Peter asked the risen Lord "What shall this man

do?" (referring to John), Jesus answered, "What is that to thee? Follow thou me."

5. So our only problem is to keep our own channels clear for our own Inner Guidance *and to follow same.*

6. We must discriminate, yes. But in an objective way, not an emotional way. "By their fruits you shall know them." So why not observe the *fruits* of various endeavors as distilled thru our own Intuition, without judging until our own Inner Guidance tells us how to cooperate with the Good?

7. "Of that day and that hour knoweth no man. No, not even the Son, but the Father only." Why then are earnest Disciples falling over each other to prophecy dates and hours?

8. "When you hear them say 'Lo here and Lo there,' go not forth. For as the lightning flashes from the East even unto the West so shall the Coming of the Son of Man be." This chimes in with our observation that the Coming of the Christ is the awakening Christ Consciousness *around the globe* today. This, as we have said, is a present fact and is increasing hour by hour. We do not deny that the recent Turning of the world Tide in the direction of the All-Good may now be greatly stimulated by the Presence of One or more Emissaries incarnated directly from the Christ Plane Who may carry the *title* "Christ." The attitude of such an emissary however is not a take-over attitude but on the contrary His or Her participating here depends entirely upon enough Christ Consciousness having been generated in members of the Race so that our free-will is, as always, sacrosanct. We *choose* the Coming of the Great One; and He or She will have to be *invited* to participate. This is the Age of *Spiritual Democracy,* not of absolutism.

9. As for His or Her "ruling," this is a concept of previous ages, not of the New Day of enlightened Individualism; and in spite of some adverse appearances, Spiritual Democracy does now prevail.

Christ is *coming*? Christ is *here*. The very Christ is *within* each of us. It is our essential nature. But how many of us are right-minded enough to receive, understand, embody *and manifest* Christ Principles?

Jesus allowed Himself to be crucified by those who wanted Him to march against Rome, thus *forcibly* "setting everything right" for "His Elect"—meaning themselves. Right-ness is a personal achievement within each of us, East or West, male or female, high or low in human society. And tho our Father-Mother God (as objectified in Galilee by Jesus Christ) will suffer and die endeavoring to *inspire* us to be and to do what we ought to be and do, yet He-She will *never* override our Individuality by forcible conquest or by Mind-Power as some mortals seem to expect. His-Her way of "ruling" is to establish a perfect Cosmic Law, under which the Individualized Consciousness has absolute freedom to advance as fast as he or she is willing and no faster. "Punishment" is merely the inevitable frustration which we bring upon ourselves by thinking and acting contrary to the Great Law, (which actually is the outpicturing of our own essential nature.)

Only as we become able to govern our Inner selves shall we receive a global Leader Who can focalize our Christ qualities in Earth terms and act as a Spearpoint for our *Heavenly* desires.

Yes we do have perfect freedom. And this is why an Individual, when perfected, has Individuality. He-She has arrived at the Kingdom of God (Self-Awareness) by developing his-her own special arrangement of the qualities of Universal Be-ing. And He-She is manifesting them in a *new* way which charms, inspires and glorifies each other Individual who is doing the same.

The Second Coming of Christ is just this. And it is a burgeoning fact today. It is the victorious surfacing of the Christ Identity of each Unit of the Life-Wave (said to be about 6½ billion souls). When we understand this, and that It is happening today *in us,* we cease to turn outside (into 3 dimensions) for our Help. We turn Within (*live* Within) for our Help and turn outside to *give*, not get. Of course we do receive from the outer also; otherwise we could not be oriented to this plane. But our outer help comes, like the Kingdom of Heaven, "not with observation" but as a result of our Inner work, which has made us so magnetic that all we need of Help and joy comes to us from both Inner and outer sources.

It is all very simple. The reason we do not do it is because of our subconscious. Deep within each of us are the fears, the diffidence, the egocentricity, and the insecurity which the Race has lived under. But these are only immaturities and can be dropped at will when our Inner Power is perceived. Does it seem like a titanic struggle? This struggle is necessary for us to develop our Creative sinews (cut our Spiritual teeth).

Every struggle is a struggle with our old, immature self, not with other people nor with things. Believe us, it is far easier to deal with your own self, alone in the night with God, than to array yourself against what *seems* like the belligerence, the coldness, or the irrationality of the Universe. The Universe is perfect—a perfect manifestation of the Love-Intelligence which is God-Almighty. So is our own manifestation perfect in the *relative* sense that it outpictures *exactly* what we have chosen to create thru previous and present lives. Our own subconscious has created false and limiting pictures in our body, mind, and affairs because we have not sufficiently used the Divine Power within us to dissolve and correct the old old superstitions, grievances, and self-will impulses which encrust every immature Son-Daughter of the Most High.

Also some of us have over-stressed the *Power* aspect of God and tried to embody this ourselves without sufficiently balancing it with the softening qualities of *Universal* Truth and Love.

We can correct our consciousness as of *now*, and acquire the ever-new, Life Giving qualities which belong to us as soon as we are able and willing to claim Them.

This is the Resurrection.

CHAPTER 2

Mother-Father God

It is a question why God in the Occidental world seems so unrelentingly masculine.

Perhaps it is because the Orient is inclined towards the feminine interpretation and the West must balance the global scale by developing the more aggressive qualities.

We believe that Jesus' conception of the Parent-Source was far above differentiation into masculine or feminine. But the "My Father" which He used is a much warmer conception than the word "Parent" would have implied; and in fact we have no word in English which can adequately carry the intimate yet transcendent implication which is needed.

Let us realize therefore that the highest Spiritual concepts cannot at present be expressed in human language. But let us by all means correct any habit we may have formed of over-balancing our concept of God on either the masculine or the feminine side.

In this New Age the writer has been given a clear Leading that since our thought creates our Universe, we must be very careful to align our highest conceptions with *exactly* what we wish to experience. The words "Our Father" are probably the most powerful words ever spoken except the statement "I AM" which constitutes the Name, or Nature, of God as given to Moses at the Burning Bush.

Our Father! At our present literal-minded stage what does this do to our subconscious? Does it overbalance our idea of Perfection on the aggressive as opposed to the receptive side of Be-ing? Observing the Occidental code of "go get it," we opine that it has done so.

There are 12 qualities which we are developing in this

cycle of our Evolvement, and we are told that six of these are masculine and six feminine. They must be developed in balance in accordance with the Christ Pattern for this solar system as modified by our Individual Purpose in this particular incarnation. As Oriental cultures have strongly emphasized the passive qualities surrounding the function of Meditation, so Anglo-Saxons have placed great emphasis on the superactive qualities surrounding the function of material accomplishment. (Material accomplishment of course is not for its own sake—the skyscrapers will pass into dust—It is merely an object lesson by which the Individualized Spirit learns the inter-relation between Principles so that It may presently project *new* Individual Centers of Christ Awareness in Life-Waves yet unborn).

We wonder if the prevailing hyper-tension in some world areas allows its devotees to become quiet at any time short of the grave. And yet the tension of outer material manifestation is a necessary correlative to our Inner Awareness. Life is a breathing process. We breathe *in* from the Infinite and *out* into objectivity. And we *learn* and *grow* thereby. Any unbalance in our development can be easily corrected. Simply stop using Spiritual concepts from a past century and think for yourself from scratch. "Our Father" is perhaps our basic Spiritual concept—and a marvelous one. But why not change this at times to "Our Father-Mother God" or "Our Mother-Father God?"

The writer has found that this balances her upward Reach. For working purposes we may think of the Father aspect as quickening our forward-reaching qualities such as the qualities involving *Idea* (the active pole of God), while the Mother aspect fills in with the balancing, healing, comforting and quieting qualities surrounding Her manifestation as Divine *Substance* (the counterpart of Divine Idea).

It is amazing how the concept of Divine Passivity (objectified as Universal ethereal Substance) reassures and quiets the hungry, striving mind and will. Divine Passivity (Receptivity) fills all space in the outward form of all-pervading Substance. There is no hole anywhere in Universal Substance. If there were, the Universe would instantly fall apart. This is the Principle behind the scientific fact that "Nature abhors a vacuum." There can be no vacuum in Universal Spirit-Substance. The Principle of Divine Passivity is all-pervasive. Striving after money? Money is the objectification of Divine Substance; and if you claim your Christ Identity as Divine Idea, which you actually *are*, then you know also that you *are* Divine Substance as well. For one of these aspects cannot exist without Its balancing opposite. In very Truth "The Lord our God is One." So Divine Idea implies Divine Substance and Divine Substance implies Divine Idea; and our nature is completely harmonized and fulfilled by this realization.

Realizing Mother-God quiets, comforts, balances and interpenetrates us with infinite Love and Security. Realizing Father-God inspires, strengthens and interpenetrates us with joyous Growth and Activity. The two conceptions converge at any point at which we fix our enlightened attention. If we fix it at the solar plexus we are completing the *conscious* polarity of the body which flows between brain and abdominal ganglia. And if we fix it mentally on the subconscious, the Superconscious will immediately flow in to Regenerate that dark and dismal area. If we fix it on Service (for the All) we immediately attract Divine Substance sufficient to manifest the *God*-Ideas which we conceive. As soon as we are truly ready to objectify Them *in Divine Order*, we find that They bring Their own Substance with Them, sufficient and overflowing.

We are told that some aspirants develop the abdominal (feminine) pole of the body before the mental (masculine) pole is greatly illumined. The Egoic Light can then be seen more in the solar plexus than in the head. There are two main Paths up the Mount of Transfiguration—the Love Path and the Mind Path, or the feminine and masculine approaches.

Whichever is developed first, the other must be evolved to make a perfect balance. Understanding this, we can work much more intelligently in our Spiritual Communion.

In the relativity consciousness which we live in on Earth, we can sometimes think of Mother-God as *underneath*, whereas Father-God is *over-all*. Do we tire of constant striving upwards? Then we realize Mother-God beneath us, assimilating, balancing, comforting and giving Rest. If we fall (either physically or metaphorically), we fall into the "Everlasting Arms" of Mother-Substance. *If we let Her*, by believing in Her, She will pick us up for another start on a higher spiral of consciousness.

> Two—
> polarity of Earth—
> Man and Woman—all and none.
> Cross-vibration causing Form,
> Both contained with the One.

So a *temporary* recognition of the *seeming* difference between Mother and Father God helps amazingly in the conscious Regeneration of our minds, souls and bodies. But this should not be attempted until we are very sure we realize that the Lord our God is forever One. This Oneness of course is the basis of our Communion (Meditation) work and it must be with us even while we are working in objectivity. Actually the masculine qualities are implied in the feminine and vice versa. It is only for purposes of particularization that we at certain points in our objectification may place the Mother qualities or the Father qualities in the forefront of our consciousness.

Mother-God may also be thought of as governing our subconscious, which, among other things, builds the body. If we ask Her She will unobtrusively work in this vast area to heal confusions and errors while our conscious attention is directed into objectivity.

It gives a general healing balance to think "I Am One

with the Lord Christ who is One with Mother-Father, Father-Mother God." Or we may go directly to our Parent-Source; "Father-Mother, Mother-Father I surrender my whole Be-ing to You for Regeneration." A tremendous Inflow will follow such a Meditation. Can we become quiet enough to receive It? We can try.

Since we Westerners have weighted our God-concepts so strongly on the masculine side, we recommend *much* quiet Communion, with the healing Mother-qualities in the forefront of our consciousness. However Communion is a Law unto Itself. The very Communion will show the seeker how best to proceed for his or her speedy healing and advancement.

Perhaps you may say that aggressiveness is *natural* to Occidentals and that they *like* the break-neck pace of our present civilization. Why then do they need such quantities of caffein, alcohol, pep-talks etc to *stimulate* them, plus so many sleeping pills, stomach pills, cigarettes and such to "quiet their nerves?"

CHAPTER 3

Be Still

As Sampson's strength was in his hair, so the strength, power, consolation and victory for the New Age citizen are in Prayer, Meditation, Dwelling in the Secret Place of the Most High, or whatever you may wish to call It. Our name for this essential activity is Communion; and yet even this cannot fully describe that most Holy state of the Individual Spirit—Its conscious recognition of the All-Goodness of Its Source, and the purposeful return to Its Healing arms.

Down the ages words take the connotation of the way they are used. The word Prayer has come to be adulterated so that it tends to mean today the ordering of what one wants—and intends to have—much as one would place an order with Sears Roebuck. The degree of Spirit and of self-surrender which the pray-er puts into this order is questionable; and consequently the degree of uplift (Answer to Prayer) is minimal.

Meditation? Meditation denotes a higher motivation than the superficial type of Prayer. When a person meditates, presumably he or she does wish to merge with the Higher (Universal) Mind-Spirit, and so to attain a deeper consciousness with which to live his life on Earth. But Meditation has come to involve a great deal of *passivity*. Some passivity is necessary on the part of the aspirant to Divine Communion. But it can be overdone. It may lead to a state of light trance, which does not help us much to rise in consciousness—i.e. to exchange our limited conceptions for the Universal ones which alone can solve our problems.

To "Dwell in the Secret Place of the Most High" is the condition which all pray-ers are (or should be) aiming for. But

13

how to arrive there? To dwell in a place, one must get there first.

So perhaps our best word for the present is Communion. This implies action both ways. We surrender our faulty or limited consciousness in exchange for the healing, purposeful Consciousness Which gave us birth as an Individual and Which knows all things—absolutely all things—concerning us and our Spiritual Evolvement.

Jesus, when He raised Lazarus, looked upwards and said, "Father I thank You that You have heard me." So He must have turned within (upwards in Consciousness) and articulated His desire to the Almighty. This being a desire for the Giving of Life, which is in line with the Father's Purpose for us; and Jesus being a clear channel for this purpose to objectify thru, the Prayer was answered and Jesus was empowered to speak the Word of actual, physical Resurrection for Lazarus.

Jesus also added; "And I knew that You hear me always; but for these I said it, that they may know that You have sent me." This proves Jesus' complete *belief* that the Father always hears us when our motive is right. Both His conscious and subconscious minds were permeated with this belief, which is the first requirement for successful Prayer.

How to arrive at this glorious state of Communion? First of course believe that there *is* a Universal Mind-Spirit infinitely higher than ours; and that It is *for* us *now*, in this moment of space and time. The only thing which can bar us from Its benificence is our own limited, timid, half-resentful or self-inflated approach. As Emmet Fox well said, we must furnish the "mental equivalent" to the Good which we expect to receive. For like attracts like thru all this Cosmos, and if we wish to ensoul the Cosmic Love-Truth-Life which is God, we must *be* these very things ourselves. We must *Love* our Mother-Father with all our Be-ing; we must desire the very *Truth* "as the hart panteth after the water brooks;" and we must be *alive* in our aspiration, not whining, half-hearted, doubtful, hurried, or with three quarters of our mind on other things.

So we accomplish Communion. We *know* that our burden has been shifted upwards. Then we must reverse the process and become *receptive*. Having analyzed our lack or our difficulty, (which analysis is for the benefit of our own subconscious, not to enlighten God), we now release it and wait for the Comfort which will surely come. Spiritually, mentally, emotionally and physically, we shall *know* that our consciousness has been raised to the point where our difficulty has been solved. Turning to other things, we shall keep this knowledge in our heart without talking about it to others. If it still bothers us, Commune again. Commune again anyway. For no mortal can withstand the pressures of this plane without many many hours of very earnest Communion. Even Jesus required it—alone, in the night usually, and sometimes all night long.

One more thing. If the Answer is "No," accept it. Never mind the why. This we shall know some day. Accept it as did Jesus in Gesthemane. Did we say that our difficulty is *always* solved? This is the solving—if the cup cannot pass, we are enabled to drink it and *like* it. Or at least we can drink it with that Inner Peace which will carry us thru it and bring us to our Cosmic Victory.

Communion is not mechanical. It is doubtful how greatly our subconscious is impressed by prayer-wheels, daily repetition of certain set phrases and such. As for God, we opine that what He-She-It looks for is the sincere upward reach of the Spirit—not the number of minutes or hours in which we repeat certain syllables given us by others and pronounced in a weary, semi-hypnotic condition.

Live Communion produces its own words—Ideas. Our "troubles"—our Spiritual lack or our excited entanglement with the psychic forces which invade Earth's envelope—are thrown upwards as we realize the All-Serenity of God plus His-Her complete but quiet assurance of the Right-ness

16

(Truth) within all situations which can possibly confront us. We were given a Pattern for Prayer which we can fall back upon when we are so confused or ignorant that we really do not know what to say. It is the Lord's Prayer. But this was given us, not as a strait-jacket, but as a springboard from which our own imaginations can soar.

At certain stages of our upward Reach, our minds may be almost out of control. Negative considerations assail us and try to take us over. Certain grievances or fears either paralyze our thinking processes or fill them with angry, self-justifying repetition of (to us) reasonable facts. In this case we can always grasp that greatest of all life-savers—"Our Father." In this condition we may have to repeat this many many times, varying it with a statement of the *nature* of this, our Saving Source; "Wholeness is Your nature." "You know the Answer to this. I open my self to You Who *are* the Answer." Of course we never forget the point of contact as being *within us* and *within all*; "Who art in Heaven (The Kingdom of Heaven is *Within*)." Remote recognition of God is powerless. Unless God is *Within* us, how can He-She *transmute* us?

Whatever comes to us to say (think) is more helpful than any set form. For instance a spontaneous remark such as "Lord Christ I Love You" will often unburden us of all our unChristlike harassment. For Love is unification; and to unite with the perfected Individual Mind of the Lord establishes our channel of Communion with the Infinite and sets us free. "I Am the *Way*, the Truth and the Life."

If a person accomplishes this, he or she will not need nicotine, caffein, alcohol, horse-racing or roulette as a "recreation" or "relaxation." Communion is the *natural* activity of Mankind. It gives Comfort, Peace, Companionship and refreshment and It gradually turns us into the attractive, deeply purposeful, able, dynamic and loving person whom we know ourself to be.

Many people fall asleep as the first stage of Communion relaxes hectic tensions in the mind. This sleep is good; for the body then builds a certain degree of peace into the organism. But what a waste! We could have spent several hours Communing; thus dissolving, not only surface difficulties, but some of the deep psychic snarls which dog our footsteps by means of the subconscious. We see therefore that this God-Activity of Communion must be our *main* occupation—not just a soul-palliative to get us out of today's petty difficulties. It must be a large part of our life activities, not just a period snatched from the necessary hours of sleep.

Our *main* occupation! What blasphemy against the great god Mammon! As everyone knows, our best energies, highest abilities, and most of our waking hours, must go to keep our family in the style to which they would like to be accustomed, to build up that bank account, go to the beauty parlor, walk the dog, wash the car, bake a cake, put our hair in curlers, soak that ankle so we can be on the job to-morrow etc etc ad ridiculosity. Modern Man's oh-so-virtuous theme-songs!

Better take this state of mind into the Great Healing Silence and courageously listen to what It says. Do we dare do that? If not, then we are putting ourselves into the mad materialistic current which is today sweeping immature souls into they know not what. If we, who know better, cannot live in the Oneness which gives us Spiritual control, how can we complain if the worldly current sucks us under against our will?

Our national coins in America say "E pluribus unum"—"Out of the many, comes the One."

We have the many (multiplicity)—things, things, things, on every shelf. Where is the One? The Principle of serene, purposeful, One-directed life? It is here, good people, if we have time and courage to go against the current and *be* It. We *are* of that Principle. We ourselves *project* our *things*. As "The Sabbath was made for Man, not Man for the Sabbath," so industrialism is for *us*, not we for it. In fact, ironically, industrialism arose for the purpose of freeing Mankind from slavery to outer necessities. In freeing the hands and the feet (to a degree) from drudgery, it appears that we are allowing it to enslave our mind, our emotions, and our Spirit as well. Of course this is entirely unnecessary. We *could* use our marvelous inventions to *enhance*, not to warp our Higher life.

Is the Race going to submit to the ridiculous situation which now exists of slavery to our own projections? If so, then the New Generation will miss the boat and be obliged to hand over its torch to other Souls capable of "bringing forth the fruits thereof." For the New Age spells Spiritual Freedom. And we can now bring forth this glorious concept *if we will*.

Our solution is to Commune Within; and to use the consequent Power of Love-Truth to solve our outer issues. But as in the case of alcoholics or other addicts, our first and worst hurdle is to *realize* that we are caught in a quagmire of psychic drag (subservience to lower desires) and to *admit* that we need major correction from our Parent-Source.

MEDITATION (Communion)
"My Spirit, my mind, my emotions, my will and
my body are aligned within the Universal Christ
Consciousness. This is accomplished by the
Grace of the Lord Christ Immanuel Who was sent
to show us how to do this; and who demonstrated
it Himself."

CHAPTER 4

Advanced Christianity

The New Age certainly embraces a new cycle in the Self-Awareness of Mankind.

But let us remember that the new Awareness, however thrilling and revolutionary, is built upon the best of the basic Principles which we inherit from previous ages. The Age just previous to ours (called by some the Age of Orthodox Christianity), was absolutely necessary as an incubator for the great Seed which was planted in Galilee and which has taken these 2000 years to sprout world-wide.

Some people "Throw out the baby with the bath." Zealous advocates of the New Cycle wish to free themselves from the literal and binding interpretations which the Old Cycle has sometimes put upon historical events. In doing so they often scorn and reject the very Principles upon which the New Age must be built.

For instance, the writer has been accused of embracing Old Wives' Tales because she retains the basic Christian Revelations which have—miraculously—survived the dark winter of the Middle Ages and been handed down to us, in allegory for the most part. It is only the narrow, crystallized and literal-minded interpretations which she rejects. The great Principles and Events remain.

Only by continuous and selfless Spiritual Communion can this confused situation be righted.

For another instance, we were once solemnly told that there never was such a Person as Jesus Christ. Well if there was not, then Someone Else said the things which electrify the open-minded soul today and explain the Mastery of Life which no one but that Person has ever even claimed to have attained. The Scripture has been garbled? Ah yes. But could

any garbler invent the Regenerating statements which shine
thru the centuries to liberate the open mind today with Light
which Mankind has never before experienced? No, nothing
but the embodied Word of Truth could speak to the centuries
as did Jesus Christ. We do not care by what name you call
Him. There was Someone Who spoke the Word of Continuous Life for *All*—the Word which we should all speak if we
were able, and the same Word which some others have *par-
tially* spoken and embodied in both Orient and Occident.

Not only did Jesus Christ *speak* this Word; but *proved* It.
Not only did He *transcend* matter (in the Ascension), as some
others are reported to have done. He alone as far as we know
deliberately *de*scended into the unredeemed areas of human
consciousness (called "death") and *rose* from that sad state,
proving His Mastery over the full Circle of our planetary
experience.

"I Am the Resurrection and the life."
"I Am the Way, the Truth and the Life."
"I Am the Light of the world."
"Before Abraham was, I AM."
"I and my Father are One."
"All Power is given unto me in Heaven and in Earth."
"My words are Spirit and they are Life."
"As the Father raises up the dead and quickens them,
        so has He given to the Son to quicken
        whom He will."

And at the end;

"I call you no longer servants but friends."
"These works that I do you also shall do and
        greater works."
"If my words abide in you, you shall ask what you
        will and it shall be done unto you."
"I ascend to my Father and to your Father and to my
        God and your God."

Did Anyone Else ever speak and prove these words?

Have you ever considered the Council of Nicaea? Almost 300 years after the Lord ascended, the early Christian churches, harassed by the persecutions of Rome, were huddled around the Mediterranean Sea with practically no inter-communication and each with its supposedly authentic manuscripts and word-of-mouth traditions. Constantine, the Roman emperor, after he saw the fiery Cross in the sky, tried to draw them together and to give their collective belief government recognition.

Perhaps no other mere human has ever had such a task as Constantine. Around the little Mediterranean cloister lay a horde of heathen stretching almost around the globe. And in the consciousness of the heathen-born emperor was no doubt a similar conflict. It is said that the forces of retrogression, bent upon destroying the New Light, ran rampant at the Council of Nicaea so that the marvel is that the Principles were preserved at all. That they were preserved, even tho largely in a casing of imagery, allegory and outer ceremonial, is proof that they had Life in themselves.

Since these Principles quicken the Spirit today as does nothing else ever uttered or acted on Earth, we see that the Lord Christ knew His Mission and planned for Its survival. It *has* survived unto this day and is now being brought into usable terms for the conscious Regeneration of all who, with a reverent Spirit, have followed the elementary character courses preparatory to the great Awakening of this time. The invitation to the Awakening is Race-wide; "Many shall come from the East and the West and sit down in the Kingdom." And conversely; "Many shall say to me 'Lord, Lord' and I shall say to them 'Depart from me. I never knew you.'"

The Bible as we have it is to be read with the Spirit, not with the material, literal-slanted *lower* mind. Furthermore, the Lord clearly said "I have many more things to tell you but you cannot bear them now. In that Day (which we believe to be *this* Day), I will tell you plainly of the Father."

The pre-Christian mind, for the most part, could not think in abstract terms. In fact the Jewish nation was one of the few groups which postulated *one* incorporeal, abstract, *Universal* God. Therefore theirs was the privilege of furnishing a channel for the advent of the Christ (or Sonship) Principle. The Christ Principle embraces, not only the concept of Universal, abstract Be-ing (God the Father-Mother), but proclaims the imminent unification of the *Individualized* Spirit (Individual Man) with This, Its *Causative* Source.

It was 2000 years before Mankind as a whole had developed abstract mind to the point where such Principles made sense to it. Consequently the deep Truths (the Sonship Truths), which were *proved* in Galilee had to be put into allegorical form, slanted to develop the *character* of the people preparatory to their acceptance of and *right use of* abstract explanations when they should become able to handle such dynamic conceptions.

We are very grateful for the work done by past centuries. But that does not mean that we countenance teachings which, tho perhaps uplifting in their right time and place, have no value save a destructive one in the great liberating Light which the mature perception of these abstract Principles now gives us. Neither do we "throw out the baby with the bath" by jettisoning the Principles in the process of casting off crystallizations which have dimmed them. The Principles, and the historic Events which proved their Reality, are the opposite of Old Wives' Tales. They are the lifeblood of the new, *scientific* generation.

Therefore we do not scorn the human aspects of the Chrismas Story, nor despise morbid emphasis on the details of Calvary spoken by those who are going thru their own Crucifixion and cannot yet realize that the Resurrection is here for the taking.

But as for a God who metes out eternal torture to His errant children, (as still maintained by some "Christians" in high places), we shudder at such a pre-Christian nightmare.

The pace of the Race's upward surge is faster and ever faster. Can we sort out the True from the false and enter the New Day rejoicing? We can try.

CHAPTER 5

The Thrust of Life

The title of this chapter tells the story. Life *is* a Thrust—
a Creative Thrust. It surges out from the Heart-Mind of
Universal Be-ing in order to develop an infinite number of
Centers of Individual Self-Awareness which can go forward
forever in their appreciation of the All Be-ing and in joyful
rapport with each other.

The three main apects of God are Life, Love and Truth.
Each Divine Center endeavors to develop these aspects within
Itself, and to harmonize them by their constant use in the
Evolvement of still greater Awareness.

Consider the salmon, for instance. He has life. Apparently
he has more Life than can be contained in his deep-sea exist-
ence. He wishes to *give* Life in the propagation instinct
·without which the March of Progress would have died as it
was borning.

But more than *simple* instinct animates the salmon. Without of course having the slightest conscious inkling of what
he is about, he puts himself into a willing attitude so that
the Odic Stream of Creativity can use him for World Service.
As the caribou's annual migration has furnished many of
the needs of the Eskimo, so the salmon's prodigious efforts
to spawn at the head of the river furnishes food for inland
humans plus we know not what of other benefits to various
animal species. Roaming is not just a useless pastime. Roaming is a legitimate function by which Nature interweaves Her
benefits among Her enormous family of creatures. Birds in
their migrations eat the seeds of plants in their southern
quarters and carry them in their intestines to Alaska or
elsewhere.

So within the All-present Cosmic Law the salmon is serving, not only his own species, but the great outer world which he knows nothing of. In this serving he displays unkowingly the Divine quality of *Love* to the final degree of often giving his life in the process. He does all these things by Law. Adapting himself to the necessities of his own life requirements he is obeying the Cosmic Law which is *Truth*, and which is the *how* of all created Expression.

Can we doubt that the Christ qualities are borning in all units of Creation? Even the cricket with his little chirp is expressing Life and the Joy thereof. Consider the salmon with his Life, Love, and Truth development; and then consider your beautiful dog. Have you not seen in her eyes the Thrust of Life,—becoming vaguely self-conscious as she nears the top of the Animal Life-Wave? She is *alive* down to the last wave of her expressive tail. She looks at you with *Love* unmistakable. She follows the great Law (*Truth*) of her Be-ing as well as she is able *and* she looks at you with perfect articulation which says "I wish to be more than I am; and I *shall* be so." Thereby she proves herself to be an evolving unit of God-Presence,—an open-ended and intelligent Spark of Self-Awareness.

It is said by scientists that even the atom, within its *very* limited gravitational field, has the Power of Choice (Self-determination). This is the hallmark of potential Christhood; and in maturing Mankind it has evolved to the point where each Individual is potentially Master of his or her own Be-ing in the twelve aspects (or faculties) which constitute our objectification on this planet.

> "Meanest worm hath sense of pleasure;
> Before God the Seraph stands."

These are words from Schiller's Ode to Joy which Beethoven put to victorious music in the chorale of his 9th Symphony. Can we say more to prove that the Thrust of Life pervades all Creation? In fact the Thrust *is* the Creation.

We are IT. And we shall be more and more and more of It as the aeons roll.

The Thrust at our present level must always include the Life, Love and Truth of our Be-ing in balanced proportion. The hallmark of their harmonious combination is Beauty. When you see Beauty, you know that at some level, the Life-Unit has balanced these three ingredients. True, at our level there may be superficial beauty of face and form encasing a rather immature or even unbalanced thought or emotional body. But observing the action as well as the outer form of any of God's creatures, you can tell whether or not it is advancing in an orderly and joyful way upon its Path of Evolvement.

Let us borrow again from your dog. Consider the phenomenon of the tail-wag. In its joyful movement it expresses Life. In its response to your caresses it expresses Love. And as it obeys the laws of harmonious form, it expresses Truth, or Law. Therefore it is beautiful. Some dogs have suffered mutilation by immature Man who breeds them for certain proportions after his own notions rather than according to Cosmic Harmony. But the natural dog has a tail which balances the whole structure and flows free to express the legitimate sentiments of the little psyche which inhabits it.

The Thrust of Life may be studied from any number of angles. Johnnie has a beautiful apple (which in itself is a Thrust of no mean calibre). His first thought, perhaps, is to give little sister a bite. This is an advanced expression of the Great Thrust. It is a voluntary Thrust of Love. Johnnie however is only at the threshold of Christ Consciousness. He places his fingers so that little sister can only secure a small piece of the delicious fruit. The Thrust of Love is not yet in full command of Johnnie's Be-ing.

"Before God the Seraph stands." It takes aeons for us to be able to stand consciously before Universal Be-ing, blameless and perfected in the Divine qualities of Life, Truth and Love. Yet we are coming closer each day if we have grasped the Principles of Spiritual Communion and are working with It constantly to harmonize our faculties in accordance with the tremendously varied but absolutely irresistible Thrust of Life within us and within all. The Pattern of the grade we are now entering upon was given by Jesus Christ Who is now Lord Christ Immanuel. As Jesus on Earth He poured out His whole earthly embodiment in a perfect Demonstration of the Life, Truth and Love which we too must perfect and practice so that we may pass It on to Life-Waves yet unaware of their Christ nature. Perhaps, much later, we shall even become Creative enough to project *new* Life-Waves in a Universe which has no limit and in which we are the beloved and glorified Sons and Daughters of the Most High.

The Thrust of Life appears in everything we do, from writing a book to eating a banana. Even in the seemingly passive project of sleep It carries us in Its own momentum. We are loth to cease sleeping until it has run its course.

Needless to say, efforts to enhance our Thrust of Life by the use of caffein or other stimulants are like over-drawing our bank account. If we spend more than we have, we pay it back—the hard way. A fine man once told me that he kept himself in debt because it enhanced his will-to-work. Obviously this was self-will speaking. Self-will is unnecessary when we know our Divine nature with its very adequate Creative Thrust. Its projects carry our soul with them and so turn out to satisfy us in a much deeper way than self-will ever can produce.

Much of our trouble stems from our habit of looking *downwards* instead of upwards for our behavior patterns; (backwards instead of forwards). "Death is inevitable because lower Life-Waves (animals and plants) always must yield up their embodiment in form sooner or later." And in our human past "There have always been wars and so there always must be." Such defeatism is disastrous. The Thrust of Life is God Almighty; and It is ever-new, ever-progressing, so that we must always forfeit our imperfect manifestations in favor of higher and higher ones. As we mature, however, we shall be able to *transmute* our body cells and pass *voluntarily* to higher planes of Expression as did Jesus in the Resurrection and Ascension. Our forcible ejection from the body in a slow, painful and humiliating process called "death" is now unnecessary in the Light of the New Age Truth.

Part II

CHAPTER 6

Are We Able?

In Glendale, California, a group of dedicated people have established a Memorial Park for the purpose of substituting the concept of Victory in place of the morbid, totally false concept which many people hold concerning the great Adventure called "death." This is Forest Lawn Memorial Park.

Walking up the open hillside you pass several beautiful but simple chapels where those who must deal with this false concept may part with the bones of their loved ones in dignity and reverence.

First of the three features which carry one up to the Victory concept is a gorgeous stained-glass reproduction of the historic portrayal of the Last Supper by Leonardo Da Vinci. This masterpiece, tho not conceived in the New Age Consciousness, yet speaks today in warm human tones and prepares you for what is to come.

Continuing up the hill (and we hope you are on foot), you come to the epic picture of the Crucifixion—200 feet long and *alive* to the last inch. Not a trace of morbidity dimmed the artist's concept. Jesus stands on the hill of Golgotha with Jerusalem in the distance. He is clothed in white and is obviously at Peace among the frantic emotions which surround Him. The various human passions of greed, malice, fear, bewilderment etc are there,—for the moment at bay before the Serenity of the Lord. Colorful, and alive beyond all expectations, this picture is truly a great Event in the life of anyone who is aware of the planetary Story.

Continuing to the top of the hill you come to the third feature—the Resurrection picture. This is the Event with which we are concerned here and which the Race is just beginning to experience Individually.

32

This artist's concept is truly inspired. He portrays, not a sunburst of total exaltation, but exactly what the Race is experiencing today and—we have no doubt—about what Jesus experienced as He first emerged from the false horror of His Earth Mission.

Tho He stands in a path of Light and the corona about His head is visible, yet He does not wholly dominate the scene. His arms are extended towards an array of white-robed figures who appear in the upper right quarter of the picture, to welcome Him and to help Him complete His Accomplishment. This is the polarity of the picture—Jesus, in His white robe, within His own golden light, reaching upwards, almost tentatively, towards His supporters On High.

In the left upper quarter heavy clouds still lower, relieved only by a rim of light breaking over the hill where three small crosses still stand. The right lower quarter is filled with arid Palestinian earth, dim and still slumbering, apparently unaware of what has occurred as the Lord emerged from His rocky tomb.

Truly a magnificent conception. And it applies to US as all Earth masterpieces must. For everything which happens here is for us—to help us understand ourselves and our Purpose here in three dimensions. Each Earth happening, small or great, portrays the constant Outpouring of that Love-Intelligence Which projects us moment by moment and Which never for an instant flags in Its efforts to help us gain our great personal Victory.

So Jesus rose in Galilee and since then, we can rise too *if we will*.

How to go about it? God will show you. Never doubt that He-She-It knows our exact status on our Path of Evolvement and sends (thru the Cosmic Law) *exactly* the experiences which will reveal to us our faulty thought-patterns and press us into the Way of Attainment which is the overcoming of our psychic snags.

Taking stock of ourselves by the Christ Pattern (which

takes courage), we see first that the average present pattern will not do for the New Age. "That man lived to be 100 years old. Isn't that wonderful?" Did he really *live*? Glory to him if he did really meet the crucial issues of a long and fruitful life on the physical-emotional levels. Doubtless he must have done so to have survived so long. But is even this good enough for the New Age? That depends on the *quality*, not the quantity of his years. Has he grasped the concept of *Continuous Conscious Life*? Does he know the ingredients necessary for the final overcoming of the death limitation? How much of eternal Truth-Love was he able to ray out to the Race thru his body, his love-nature, and his work? Did he surrender self-will in the cause of Universal Service? And finally, did he know the great Truth that he who would save his life shall lose it whereas he who is willing to yield it up "for my sake and the Gospel's" shall save it unto Life Eternal?

Perhaps he did know these things to a degree. But who except the Lord Christ has so far on Earth known *and done* them *completely*?

We are not belittling the man who survived for 100 years. We are merely saying that in taking stock of our own selves we wish to clarify our objective, setting our goals and en-quiring *constantly* Within as to our most expedient way of arriving at Eternal Life (Continuous *Conscious* Consciousness).

Can we heal the sick, inspire the flagging, cast out demons? (Can we even *recognize* the demons when they come in the subtle, slick guise of what is called "common sense"?) Can we raise the dead (both the physical and the moral dead)? And can we say at our last Gesthemane when yet another and worse crucifixion looms in our path—can we say as Jesus did on that last dark night "Father I should like to get out of this. All things are possible to You. If possible get me out of it. Never-theless if You say to go thru with it, I will do it"? Can we? If we can, then ours is Life Eternal *here* and *now* and we shall experience the Resurrection forever.

CHAPTER 7

Then Let's Go

O.K. We believe we are able.

Or at least we believe that we have grasped the conception and recognize it as what we have striven for these thousands of years. We know it can fulfill us as nothing else can possibly do. If we cannot accomplish the complete Resurrection in this lifetime, we know we would rather die trying than to muddle along, hoping for some vicarious Salvation which shall align our whole Be-ing to the Reality of Life without much Spiritual effort on our part.

We also believe that there is absolutely nothing at all in our thought patterns or our emotional patterns which we are not willing to evaluate and to scrap if necessary in order to remove the blocks which bar us from our highest Self-hood.

So then, how do we really like ourself at this point in our Evolvement? Well, we find ourself not too bad according to the prevailing standard. In fact we do not know of any *outstanding* errors. Or do we? What standard are we judging by? The standard of the Age just passing, propped up by the social code and a *smattering* of the 10 Commandments? Or the standard of the New Age which the Lord Christ exemplified and bade us follow even unto death?

We have been told by self-styled New Age prophets that we must "think positive." This slogan, like all quick, pat answers to life's issues, can be misused and *is*, by superficial minds. "If I don't think well of myself, who is going to?" "For my *family's* sake I must join the worship of Mammon in my business attitudes instead of putting Principle first." "I must use *Common Sense*." "I must *smile* on all occasions."

These and many other attempts at "thinking positive" are

34

based on the glorification of self-will. The Will is one of the 12 Divine faculties of Man. But like all our other faculties it must be *Christified*. When *self*-will has the bit in its teeth the harmony of the Individual's life-picture is disrupted and the whole body becomes tense and apprehensive. Thinking affirmatively in general is an excellent habit *provided* that our thinking and our subsequent will-ing stem from *Universal* (Divine) premises, not egocentric ones.

Providing for families is an *elementary* step out of egocentricity, which even animals observe to a degree. It is *not* an excuse for scrapping highest Principle; and if we know the Truth we know that the sacrifice of Principle works in reverse even from the *material* point of view. For the Universe (including us) is governed by Divine Order (Cosmic Law). *No one* beats the game; for "the mills of the gods grind slowly but they grind exceeding small."

As for the sanctity of "common sense" (in the superficial interpretation of the term), how does this ethic stand up against such Bible injunctions as "He who would save his life shall lose it; but he who will lay it down for my sake and the Gospel's shall save it unto Life Eternal"? It is our private opinion that "common sense" as piously advocated by some, is merely another term for dear old self-interest.

And as for the perennial *smile*, please bear with us if we question it. A smile is surely an Angelic thing; and the Regenerated face will certainly contain a built-in expression of happy Serenity and good-will. But the all-conquering grin which our success courses advise us to plaster on *from the outside* is something else again. In our success magazines one can hear the camera man advising his subjects to "Say 'cheese'" as he snaps them. This, we submit, does not convey the Angelic quality which the Regenerated Individual is entitled to.

"If I don't think well of myself who is going to?" Answer; "Nobody, unless you *are* the things which you pray and preach about."

36

What about the worship of Mammon in general as a gambit for worldly success? Well, money which is gained by will-power has a way of evaporating or of becoming a bane instead of a Blessing. The person who follows this code usually becomes utterly confused. He or she realizes dimly that he has missed the boat of truly rich living, and, unwilling to admit his own error, becomes deeply suspicious of God's arrangements for Man and takes refuge in superficiality, pleasure-seeking, drink, dope, excessive TV, or some other escapism—even sometimes to the point of suicide. Meantime, tho his family may have dollars to spend, he has deprived them of deep Peace and of real, inner Security.

The foregoing are only slight hints of how our preliminary self-analysis may proceed. Actually, each Individual who has been touched on the shoulder by the Master Hand will find his or her own way to dissolve the self-illusion which many people live by. Without condemning ourselves, we come to the conclusion that we may have got by in the curriculum of the previous Age but we are only freshmen in the college course which the New Age offers.

This examination of ourselves is our first big hurdle. If we pass it we shall avoid that most terrible of all human ditches—the misuse of the Spiritual Power.

Many many eager souls pick up the New Age Revelation of the potential Inner Mastery. But not having really ensouled the lessons of character-perfection and of recognition of the Universal All-Good, which were given in the previous Age, they are still so self-centered that the discovery of their own Power leads them to self-worship. Consequently they automatically fall into the malignant error of using the Power for self-interest. Assuming that others do not know what they have discovered, they use the Divine Stream to "get ahead"—in other words to trample upon the Self-hood of others. This is one major cause of the lurking panic which haunts us today in a generation where there is but *no* excuse for anything less than Peace and Plenty for *all*. It is jungle law raised from the (comparatively harmless) physical level to the Mind level; and it is causing such severe psychic confusion in the world that our whole economic set-up is in danger.

There are many gleams of Light shining thru our present distressful situation however. And these are coming without a trace of the sanctimonious covering which has made Principle unpalatable to many honest souls in the Age just passing. Principle is one of the seven main aspects of God. It is Life-giving, not binding. It is a joy to every healthy-minded person, not a wearisome duty imposed by a stodgy society.

Young people today reject many of the Race's superficial idols. They strike to the heart of hypocrisy in their forthright psychological analyses. And these they throw about in an appealing, human sort of way. They sometimes place honesty above *superficial* politeness, which is an excellent priority.

Take for instance some of the common expressions of the new generation. Modern slang is pithy, non-pious; but deep, to the point, and to use one of our best new words "unflappable." (By this we mean that young people are "not about" to be "pushed around.")

"So what?"	"Don't kid yourself."
"Says who?"	"I couldn't care less."
"He's a stuffed shirt."	"Do your own Thing."
"It turns me off."	"We've got it made."

Do these not wield a strong arm against the outworn fetishes of a passing Age? And do they not denote a burgeoning but moderate self-confidence which refuses to be bull-dozed by categorical maxims of defeatism?

The New Age is a Democracy. Each of us is an integral part of this picture and has a deep responsibility to participate at the highest level of which we are capable. We can best help by "doing our own Thing," rather than by lending our abilities to forces of regimentation. So let us have the courage to contribute our own special Creative talents to the general Good. Yes, it will take courage—plus all the other qualities we can muster.

Do these considerations not change our appraisal of ourselves from a self-satisfied to a more elevated level? If they do, then we have some scrapping to do of our old standards and values. That great faculty of Man—Discrimination—which is objectified physically in the liver, has some mammoth work to do. And its partner—the faculty of Elimination—centered in the lower bowels, must work overtime to eliminate our outworn thought-patterns and to cleanse our ego of its tendency to grasp and hold by will-power that which does not belong to us by Right-of-Consciousness.

Speaking of the body, and along the lines of the *correct* interpretation of that great slogan "think positive," we take a hint from Myrtle Fillmore, co-founder of the world-wide Unity movement. Myrtle, in her original "miraculous" healing, stated that she spoke to her legion of body cells, apologizing to them for having given them erroneous premises to work from, and explaining that she now realized the all-perfect, Life-giving nature of our Parent-Source and would henceforth give them only workable, constructive instructions as to their natures and functions—all of which are conceived in Perfection.

As a result, her sad and degenerating organism was healed and she lived a long and glorious life on Earth and is reputed to have passed *voluntarily* to higher grounds of Activity.

So we too may begin our new life chapter by Communing constructively with our body cells, which are after all the basis of our well-being or otherwise in all our experiences on Earth.

Having Communed upwards (Inwards) with our Infinite Source, we can daily turn outwards, realizing our Mastership in the Temple of our own body, and explaining the situation to the confused array of our body intelligences. We tell them that, due to our Spiritual immaturity, we have given them erroneous concepts of life and we now wish to correct these. Instead of holding subconsciously the grim verdict that Man is born to die and that the glorious organization of our body can flourish only a few years and then must slide agonizingly into dissolution, we reverse the verdict—completely and absolutely. We tell them that our consciousness can and shall be renewed daily by our perfect Source unto Eternal Life; and that we shall vivify each cell, nerve, tissue, organ and bone by constant appreciation of its necessary function and by realization of its harmony with the rest of Creation. Thus we electrify these faithful servants with our own Divine Purpose and assure them of better and better things to follow both on this Earth and in higher spheres. In short we assure them that the Lord is come.

So our personal battle is well begun and we gird ourselves for revolutionary action.

CHAPTER 8

Scientific Communion

Since we are now praying scientifically, not just in a blur of emotion, let us shape in our minds exactly what it is we are asking for. Also we wish to align our several bodies mentally in proper sequence so that the Odic Stream of Creativity may flow smoothly down from On High and thru our lower vehicles in Divine Order.

The *tone* of our mind, not just the syllables of our words, shapes the Answer to our Prayer. A set sequence of words may mean nothing in particular to our Inner Self and therefore will evoke an Answer of nothing in particular. *We* shape our destiny by the composition of our mind, which motivates our emotions and our actions. (That is, it *should* motivate our emotions. But all too often the emotions motivate the mind, which is one of the basic troubles of our immaturity.) As an early New Thought pioneer once said "People are *always* praying and *all* their Prayers are answered." So watch what your mind is doing in its spare time.

The pattern of our mind shapes our destiny. But our mind is fathoms deep. Only the top layer is conscious with most people at this time. And even this is not yet fully liberated.

We have not yet fully exercised our God-given Power of Choice. Consequently even our conscious mind is still swayed by misconceptions from the past which assail us from events, from friends, and from the eight Authorities which we mention in a later chapter. As for the *sub*conscious, it has received such a mass of conflicting impressions from previous lives that it is a quagmire of confusion and crystallization into which we scarcely dare to look.

Take for instance the explanation of the fundamental Christ quality of Faith which an honest little girl gave in all sincerity. "Faith" said the little girl "is trying to make yourself believe something you know isn't true." Obediently she had been trying to impress her subconscious with illogical maxims which the strictly logical subconscious had been intelligent enough to try to reject.

In Spiritual Communion we are free. If we rise to a level of conscious union with Universal Spirit, we start free and clear to formulate our requests and to rid our house of the confusions, primitive urges, and emotional thinking which encrust us. One of the first acts of Jesus' Ministry was the cleansing of the Temple; "My House shall be called a House of Prayer but you have made It a den of thieves." Harsh, commercial, bargaining attitudes must go; and if the Lord (our Higher Self) does not cast them out, they will have to be destroyed the hard way—by fiery tribulation. The Reality of us and of the Universe is *free* Giving and gracious Receiving—not fear-filled grabbing on the part of the "strong" and abject submission on the part of the weak.

Would it not be well then, since we are asking Divine Mind to Regenerate our Be-ing, to have a clear idea of just what our objectified Be-ing consists of?

We have a body. "Please heal my body." We have only a slight conception of what is wrong with our body because much of it is functioning below our conscious ken. Furthermore we have only a slight conception of what our Regenerated body *should* be like. Perhaps we have not dared to rise very high in our ambitions since that would have been considered presumptuous by those who assure us that we are irretrievably created in "dust" and born in sin and must therefore suffer and die. In opposition to this, our *smattering* of Truth tells us that our body is shaped and sustained by our thoughts and emotions and that therefore we have the full responsibility for its Regeneration. What a contradiction! Then there is the soul to take into consideration. Yes, we know a bit too much to ask for bodily Regeneration without reference to our soul, our thoughts, and our emotions. How do they fit together? Where to begin? Is it presumptuous for us to try to analyze our Be-ing? God knows all. Let Him-Her do the figuring. No wonder that the old-fashioned Prayer often ends in futility when attempted by a borning citizen of the New Day!

Our Esoteric friends tell us that the next plane above the physical is the Emotional Plane (the Astral). Above that is the Mental Plane and above that the three Planes of Spirit. How do they function together? Where do we stand? And what is our correct approach to Universal Mind-Spirit?

If we did not have the eternal Pattern of the great Lord's Prayer we might fumble a long time before Divine Order is established in our Communion work. But we do have It and can fall back upon It while reaching at the same time for additional specific facts to explain ourselves to ourselves and to make our Prayers confident, scientific and enjoyable.

We begin at the top; "Our Father-Mother, Mother-Father." As we think this concept we rise into Awareness of Universal Spirit. An expression of Love and Appreciation then unifies us with this concept; "You are All and You are All-Good." "Please heal my body." There we are again. We know by now that the Odic Stream must flow down (out) thru the three planes of Spirit, down thru the Mental Plane, the Emotional Plane, and into the physical body. Therefore we might say (think) "I yield up to You my Spirit, my mind, my emotions and my body," (in that order). "I open *all* of myself to You because I trust You and wish to exchange my limited consciousness for Your Universal Awareness. I do this in the Name (nature) of the great Lord Christ Immanuel because I accept the Pattern which He showed us of the Universal Christ Individualized; and I wish my Individual Christ Identity to be fulfilled perfectly within that Pattern."

Some such Communion as this will clarify for us exactly

what it is we are desiring. God does not need enlightenment as to our state of mind. But our subconscious does; and sometimes our conscious mind does also.

Now we become passive and soon feel the beautiful Inflow of Divine Response Which is inevitable *if* we furnish the mental equivalent for the Creative Word of God to flow thru us. We continue the Communion as long as we feel able and then know surely that our Spirit is adjusted to the Universal Christ and to the Plane of our Universal Father-Mother God. Therefore the Odic Stream must flow down thru our Spirit, our mind, our emotions and our body and into our whole life-picture.

Where does the soul come in? There is much confusion surrounding this word. We can only say that a person thru Scientific Communion can receive Enlightenment from On High concerning any phase of his or her Be-ing and its relationship to God. To some "the soul" means the subconscious. To some it seems to be synonymous with the Individual Christ Spirit. To us it means the sum-total of our many life-times of lessons as distilled by our Higher Self—the over-all experience of our Individual Spirit as It has travelled thru objectification *plus* the conclusions (Principles) which It has arrived at.

Before our Spiritual maturity, many of our soul's conclusions are *wrong* from the Universal viewpoint. For instance, in Shakespeare's great psychological drama "Hamlet," Hamlet's father embraced the primitive race-code of *revenge*. From the next world he harried Hamlet to wreak vengeance on his murderer. Hamlet was too far advanced to accept this tribal principle readily; and he was torn between his own soul's higher Intuition and the parental influence. This is how our soul becomes defiled—when we do not ensoul *and follow* the highest Principle which we are capable of cognizing. Hamlet mushed along in an agony of indecision and finally killed both the offending uncle and himself, leaving the state without an heir, his fiancee with a broken heart, and plunging his own soul into a psychotic state of ambivalence which in real life it would have taken him lifetimes to unravel.

Jesus spoke of the possibility of "losing one's soul." We assume that He referred to the possible loss of the *work* the Individual Spirit has accomplished during Its long objective Evolvement, terminating in certain conclusions which Its abstract mind has arrived at and which the soul has embraced.

In our diagram accompanying chapter 12, we show the soul as located in the lower area of the Plane of Individualized Spirit (Individualized Consciousness); and we have referred to this lower area as the Soul Plane. To lose one's soul would then amount to the rejection by the Individualized Spirit (our Higher Self) of Its Evolutionary work. We are not arbitrary about this but we do feel certain that the Individual (Christ) Spirit is eternal and can never be lost even tho It may be obliged to discard the objective conclusions (principles) which Its lower self has arrived at in its Evolutionary journey.

Strictly speaking then, we believe that the word "soul" should not be capitalized as it is not the eternal Spirit but an adjunct of that Spirit.

Such questions will clear up as we go along. Suffice it to say that the more self-knowledge we have, the more quickly and painlessly and completely shall we accomplish our Regeneration and be free in body, emotions, mind and Spirit.

What about praying for our friends? *Be careful*! Are we praying *for* or *against* them? *Worrying* is highly fashionable; but highly injurious to the one we love. It is the *opposite* to Prayer. Worry says "This is terrible and I'm quite sure it's going to get worse." True Prayer *turns to God* and says "God please make this whole situation *right for everyone concerned.* You can; and I know You will if we furnish the mental equivalent. So please cause us all to see the All-Goodness of the Reality and to allow ourselves to be permeated by It *in all ways.* I ask this particularly for Eleanor at this point in her experience."

Let's be very careful to turn worry into Prayer at all costs. Worry is the *opposite* of Healing Prayer.

Of course we must be on our guard also against that common pitfall "God please make Eleanor do what I think she ought to do." When we find ourselves praying that so-and-so will do such-and-such, *there it is.* We have caught it in cold blood. *Never* should the power be used to co-erce another soul except for such a freeing statement as Jesus used *when He was invited to do so*; "I will. Be thou whole." Of course "wholeness" means "in accordance with your own Christ Identity, not *my* idea of what you should be or do.

Even to pray for a person's life (on Earth) may not always be legitimate unless he or she has asked us to do so. Perhaps he *wants* to pass over, and perhaps it is right for him to do so at this point. However it is always legitimate and helpful for us to say "Father I ask that Eleanor should know her best and Highest Way at this point in accordance with her own Christ Identity."

The manifested Universe is composed of Rhythm. Rhythm is part of the Music of the Spheres which is a building block of Form. Therefore we can deeply impress our subconscious with a rhythmic verse which can be used while washing dishes or mowing the lawn. For instance;

> Thank You Father for this day;
> And thank You that I'm on my Way.

This too is *Scientific* Communion.

CHAPTER 9

Our Karmic Past

As we survey our personal scene in our first emergence from Spiritual irresponsibility, we may see many facets of our life which do not seem to belong to us. We may find ourselves on the "wrong" side of the map, or even on the "wrong" side of the globe from what we feel would be our perfect location. We may be married to the "wrong" person, in the "wrong" work, or over-obligated to our family in some respects.

These "wrong" situations are probably old karmic debts. One big reason we have come to Earth is to work thru these even tho they may seem to hamper our true Creative Life.

There are two ways of dissolving our karma. One is to suffer thru it, subconsciously hoping that some "miracle" will set us free. Since the "miracle" may involve the death or misfortune of some person, this is not a healthy state of mind. But the urge of the ego for freedom is very strong and usually the full implication of its hopes are hidden from the conscious Self. Consequently a subconscious feeling of guilt may result.

All this is unnecessary. Karma does not have to be suffered thru indefinitely for a citizen of the New Age. Better by far of course to suffer it thru than to escape into unreality such as addiction to the various mild or not-so-mild vices which hamper our progress today. But the best and safest way to satisfy the great Law of Karma is by Spiritual Communion. Many many hours of Spiritual Communion (preferably in the night) will dissolve the obligation which created the karma. Probably some injustice was done in previous lives (either done by us or suffered by us and not forgiven). Therefore the Lord's Prayer with special emphasis on the Forgiveness Clause (both ways) will undo the damage, set us free, bless the other person and lift the Race a trifle on its upward spiral.

Frequently karmic debts coagulate into knots of psychic involvement which may include many people. These knots are usually sugar-coated with platitudes, such as may occur in old and proud families where each new member is assumed to owe life-allegiance to traditions of mutual benefit at the expense of the rest of Humanity. We have perhaps tied ourself to this by consenting to it in ages past and by pressing newborn souls into the same groove. The best way to correct this is by diligent Spiritual Treatment (Communion). Knowing ourselves to be free Sons and Daughters of the Most High we claim our freedom, asking Forgiveness for our previous allegiance to self-interest and—here is the rub—giving out *complete* Forgiveness to *all* who have pressed *us* into this mold since Man was first given Spiritual responsibility.

When we stop to think of it, every person who is below us on our Path of Evolvement has injured us by thrusting egocentric ideas into the Race-mind, many of which we take on before we are born. Thus we find that the roots of our troubles go very deep. Mass Forgiveness is therefore in order. But, conversely, we have done the same during *our* immaturity to those higher up the Path than we are. We have automatically increased the binding mass of limited conceptions thru which *they* had to struggle as we are struggling today. So we see why the Forgiveness injunction is double-barrelled and why it is the core of Jesus' Teaching—placed in the very center of the titanic Lord's Prayer.

Forgiveness means "giving *for*" as opposed to "drawing *from*" our old adversaries. This drawing from (or detracting from) we have automatically been doing by subconscious resentment. Instead of this, we now give freely to their welfare as we were intended to do to all of God's creatures.

Of course we do not consent to the error we thought we saw in them. We merely set free the Spiritual Entity whom we associated with it.

We are told that God forgives in the ratio of 1000 to 1. This is clear from the parable of the man who had his large debt forgiven by his landlord but who throttled his fellow-servant for not paying him a very small one. It is hard for us to realize at first that we really owe God the $1000 as compared to the $1 which our antagonist owes us. It actually seems to be the other way around. But as we grow in Spiritual experience we do see that much of our subconscious thinking and a great deal of our conscious reasoning and emotional motivation have been against God, the *Universal* Life, *Universal* Love and *Universal* Truth. Most of it has been for *self*, tho perhaps slightly expanded to include family, or at times, even nation.

In working to dissolve our karma, we do not imply that we should dodge responsibilities such as babies or aged parents. But if we have truly released *everybody* from our inborn possessiveness, we find that karmic debts dissolve in a very pleasant way for *all*. For freedom belongs to us as soon as we have truly given up *partial* loyalties and stepped into the Wholeness of *Universal* Service.

Our ignorance of Spiritual standards has indeed caused us to expand our indebtedness to God enormously. So we now do ask His-Her Forgiveness—which we *can* receive—in the ratio of 1000 to 1 as compared with what others may owe us.

Jesus denied His blood relationship. "Who is my Mother?" He did not allow family opposition to impede His Mission. If He had, where would we be today? It is probable that the entire Life-Wave would have failed and crashed. Yet He waited until His Spiritual maturity (about 30 years) before He claimed His Freedom. We are today Jesus' agents; and on every page of the Gospels comes the vibrant invitation "Follow me."

These and all other matters will come clear to each of us step by step *provided* we *live* in the Secret Place of the Most High and meet each outer challenge with Wisdom, knowing that it is a relic from the past and that as we deal with it the enlightened way and then release it into limbo, we form a pattern in the ethers which will benefit the whole Race forever.

We see from the foregoing that we have a mammoth job on our hands in taking up our New Age citizenship. A luke-warm attitude will not do. "I will spew thee out of my mouth because thou art neither cold nor hot." The writer has been told "I don't *object* to Jesus." Or "I don't mind *looking over* your Spiritual recommendations." Unless a person is fully convinced that a dynamic New Age is actually upon us and that the Pearl of Great Price is to be sought *and found* for our very Spiritual survival, how can he or she possibly measure up to the rigorous self-cleansing which is required? Probably the reason Mary Magdalene was the first to see the Resurrection was because she *cared* with her whole Be-ing. "Her sins, which are many, are forgiven; for she *loved much*." Loving much, we are actually *hurt* by every wrongdoing (our own or that of others) against the glorious Wholeness which is the Reality of Be-ing and which indeed is our God. Those who are ready *know* that the hour is sounding in which wrongdoing can be eradicated. "My sheep hear my Voice."

Jesus Himself *participated* on Earth. He did not just sit on a mountain and philosophize. He *cared*. People who do not follow Him into the Spiritual slums of their own Be-ing will come to a dead end sooner or later. Do not be afraid that *your* particular karma is too too sordid for you to tackle. "There is more joy in Heaven over one sinner who repents than over the 90 and 9 who need no repentance."

CHAPTER 10

Karma Reversed

Karma reversed gives richness of soul. We refer of course to *adverse* karma. *Favorable* karma already *is* richness of soul. It speaks of old situations victoriously overcome.

The narrative of our past is the narrative of our human relations. Consider if you please the many many lifetimes in which each of us has spun his web of weal and woe; of high exaltation and/or morbid sense-satisfaction or self-aggrandizement. Consider the thousands of personalities who have been involved in our hair-raising attempts at self-fulfillment,— many of which attempts were made without benefit of Higher Thought or of altruistic emotion beyond the lower Primate level of development. Is it any wonder that we come today to the Clearing House of the New Age with adverse karma assailing us from many angles and a very inadequate set of working principles in our thought-patterns with which to deal with it? Even with good intentions in our more recent incarnations, we still have that deep, treacherous mass of subconscious impulses to recognize and to conquer.

What philosophy is capable of dealing with them? None. It takes a higher Principle than the intellectual to comprehend and act upon the psychological and moral tangles in which our soul has snarled itself. Reason is *not* Man's highest faculty. Reason operates from a given premise. What Faculty is capable of comprehending *all* the factors in our soul-situations and so establishing a perfect premise? None but Universal Spirit—our Father-Mother God with Whom we are essentially One. Even Jesus said that He could of Himself do nothing. It was His Father within Him Who did the work. But at the end He said "I and my Father are One," thus announcing that He had succeeded in opening His mind, will, and other faculties to Universal Spirit, Which is now able to flow thru Him into a perfect manifestation of Itself.

Now that we too have grasped the immanence of Spirit (Universal Life, Truth, Love) in *our* Individual Consciousness, we know that our minds *can* have correct premises to reason from and that a great many of our former conclusions must be reversed or modified if we are to experience a life-picture commensurate with our highest desires. This reversal involves an arduous and courageous house-cleaning of our subconscious—so arduous that many are afraid even to uncover the portholes to see what is underneath.

The Universe has a Plan. We are not just floating. We are far, far from static. As the planets sweep constantly in perfect but very complex Order, so Individual Man sweeps along in the Life-Stream of his Race, which is coordinated with the Cosmic movement, and always advances towards greater Individual self-expression and perfection. If a star should decide to stand still, it would immediately be bumped from the rear and shattered into stardust. And if an Individual of any Life-Wave decides to just take a ride, he too is shattered by advancing forces. Of course his real Egoic Spark cannot be damaged. But his work—or outer manifestation—can be, and is, to the degree that he defies God's Law of Progress and so gives himself over to the action of Nature's scavengers. He is then the victim of *de*structive elements and suffers severe set-back in his Evolvement.

We cannot stand still. So in this New Age we had better do our house-cleaning (redeem our subconscious), and be ready for new and better activities.

Does neighbor Elsie seem to stand still and get away with it,—apparently coasting on the good-will of others and taking a frivolous view of this great Opportunity of Earth-life? Does that poor demented alcoholic seem bent on destroying himself and others and still survive? Do people in public places misuse the Divine Power entrusted to them by their constituents? Do innocent babies come to grief?

Rest assured, there is perfect Justice. There is also perfect

Mercy when that is earned by the Individual by a change in attitude. Humans are unbelievably complex and we do not see all the pluses and minuses. Only the Karmic Angels know exactly what the score is. And only they know the terrible grief which dogs the footsteps of errant mortals even tho they may for a time laugh off their subconscious fears and appear to be riding high.

Indeed a Spiritually knowledgeable person does not feel resentment at any wrong-doing, nor horror at any penalty which he sees someone obliged to pay. It is *God's* Universe and His-Her Laws are merciful beyond our dreaming. They are perfectly carried out too; and the higher planes are filled with compassionate zeal on the part of millions of Beings engaged in karmic and evolutionary work. Compassion is in order on our part; but never indignation when we witness a heavy karmic situation.

Also—and this strikes home to mortals just emerging into Universal Love—there is the parable of the workers who were hired at the 11th hour and paid as much as the all-day workers. Does this pinch a little for us as it did for the ones in the story? Do we think "God why are You so easy on him and so hard on me?" Perhaps we do. But we know better. Are we not engaged in World Service? And does this not mean that our whole Life-force is bent upon mitigating the effects of wrongdoing and on making things easier for new generations than they have been for us? Of course it does. and this is the Love of which we were composed and are composed. So we accept what higher Life-Waves do for us and we are learning to pass out the same to less mature Individuals. Our history is the story of our human relations. Our karma consists of our record regarding our human associations, which depend of course upon our understanding of God and of ourselves. Now that this understanding is being perfected (to a degree at least) we turn about to correct the psychic tangles which our immature behavior has precipitated. Every human contact we meet on Earth may be a karma. And if some of our associations are less than joyous, let us work night and day to dissolve the difficulty. Only thus can we obtain our freedom.

We should never regret our dire experiences. Our adverse karma is our opportunity to reverse volcanic situations, and so to garner that richness of soul and Spirit which constitutes our Individual joy in life.

As for that "injustice" of "innocent" babies coming to grief, please bear with us but there are practically *no* innocent babies. All except a *very few* Race Avatars come here to work out encrustations of karmic debt which can best be met by this arduous soul-course. The course *can* result in our very speedy Advancement if we understand what we are doing.

Of course karmic debts include also errors of *omission*, which are manifold and must be corrected by affirmative *Universal*-minded action.

Even to scratch the surface in studying the great Laws of karma would take lifetimes. This is so because each person in the Life-Wave is a new Creation with infinite complexities, plus free-will to develop them at his or her own pace. But a very slight knowledge of karmic situations will free us from a sense of injustice or irrationality in the Universe. We no longer pout over seeming favoritism on the part of Cosmic Law. There is no favoritism. So we can release others into Its completely competent hands and spend *all* our Creative power solving our own karma and giving out whatever surplus of Good we may have at our disposal. As Emmet Fox teaches, karma is all-pervasive, not just an Oriental phenomenon. BUT "Christ is Lord of Karma." Operating thru us, the Christ Consciousness cuts karmic knots and sets us free forevermore.

Clearing these personal tangles by Spiritual Communion will take most people some time. But this time is as nothing compared with the lifetimes we should otherwise have to traverse in order to set our house right. We are really giving ourselves Spiritual psychiatry, which is the greatest thing we can do for ourselves.

In the next chapter we shall endeavor to point out a few

of the more general psychic difficulties which beset the Race and which confront this generation. It is we who are responible for the opening of the New Age; and as Napoleon said "Generations are watching us from yonder mountain tops." So they are—in a much greater sense than we have any idea of. If enough of us set the pace for a complete acceptance of *advanced* Christian Truths, we can greatly bless the New Day. If this is not done—decisively—*now*, we shall lose the greatest Opportunity which has ever been given to the Race.

We do not claim that the process of Regenerating the subconscious will be otherwise than agonizing for most people. Discouragement, fear, grief, loneliness and despair may be our portion for some time. But never boredom. Never a sense of purposelessness. And always—but always—there will be that deepest of all assurances—that we *are* worthwhile Beings, not just pawns of an irrational Universe.

Also we realize that the great Cosmic Principle of Order has brought us to this stage of our education knowing that we are now capable of dealing with ourselves. With each Victory that we gain, this soul-strength will increase and the Joy of the Lord become ours. The all-day laborers will be glad that they suffered the "heat of the day" with the Lord, since it gives them a depth of Individuality which is theirs forever and which is the basis of their own special Creativity.

The Great Law always throws up our karmic debts to us in Divine Order—never more than we can handle at one time. In short, we are deeply cared for; and this stage of our development is necessary to us for this is how we *grow*.

The Name of the Lord Jesus Christ is all-powerful on the psychic levels. So call constantly for His Help and you will never be disappointed.

CHAPTER 11

Eight Authorities

In the Age just passing, Man has lived under 8 Authorities. These were necessary in his immature state and still are
necessary and desirable, tho in a somewhat modified form.
On the whole they have functioned well in that they have
brought us to this dawning Era in which Individual Enlightenment is the underlying Authority. This is Spiritual
Democracy; "I will write my Laws in their *hearts*." This
Bible verse was once quoted to an eminent attorney with
results which left no doubt as to what the orthodox think
of such a presumption. However, this does not mean of
course that we shall downgrade our civil law but on the
contrary that the attitude of lawlessness shall cease and every
person will live in a *lawful* state of mind, desiring only what
is right and just for everyone.

Authority No 1. Before a child is born, it is stamped,
permeated and imbued with the precepts of its forebears.
By the acceptance and repetition of these precepts down the
ages, the subconscious of our good ancestors had become
unenquiring as to their validity until, like a bolt out of the
blue, comes a New Age child who turns his or her fresh gaze
upon them and finds them wanting—for the Age which is
to be.

Take for instance the precept "noblesse oblige." This
noble sentiment has become a maxim of many of the "best
families" from the Middle Ages on down. Tho they no longer
write it on their shields, they do still carry it in their subconscious. A very inspiring principle. But imperfect in its
premise. It really means "Since we are superior to others,
we must act as such." Tho the "superior to others" may have
served as an upward impulse to Primitive Man, yet in the

Kingdom of Heaven it has no place. And unless we arrive quite shortly at the first stages of the Kingdom of Heaven *on Earth*, such separative principles will cause dear Mother-Earth to fly into trillions of uncohesive fragments.

Similarly, most of our ancestral maxims are compounded of both Truth and error confined together in a strait-jacket which leaves almost no room for the Individual conscience.

Our second Authority, which the young child soon observes, is School. What a wonderful world he now steps into—wherein he is given the power to read, to figure, to know how to do things and to get along with other people. It truly is so—or was. Nowadays we wonder. But on the whole Education has done wonders for the liberation of the human mind into the implementation of its ideas, with all the material fruits which accrue from this wonderful development.

Does Education at present give us our Heritage of *Spiritual* Truth? On the whole we can only say that at its best it has tried to liberate our intellects so that we could rationally search for these Truths. We verily believe that the Truths themselves are not known to many of our Educators. The educated intellect is often very loth to admit that there is anything higher than itself; and we are of the opinion that many of our respected intellects have not yet reached the John-the-Baptist stage of development. As Jesus said, John the Baptist was among the greatest men "born of Woman." Yet "He that is least in the Kingdom of Heaven is greater than he." But John the Baptist *admitted* his inadequacy and constantly stated "There cometh One mightier than I."

Would that all intellectuals would say the same.

Our third ancestral Authority is the Church. Children pick up Truths from hymns and sermons, which drop into their little subconscious minds and are the breeding grounds for future attitudes. Children absorb the *Power* aspect of God with alacrity and often in a very literal-minded way. "Crown Him with many crowns" for instance evokes to the Occidental mind in its immature years a ridiculous picture of a pile of crowns atop a Head with which, to be honest, they are not in the least familiar—nor do they care to be. True, they are taught that Jesus loved little children. But that was long long ago and as of *now* the picture remains of a Person Who sits under a pile of crowns and Who seems a bit remote to say the least. The hymn goes on to explain further that the crowns pertain to "the Lamb upon His Throne." Entirely ignorant of the Jewish imagery of the Sacrificial Lamb; and not particularly impressed by the ancient symbology in the first place, this explanation turns us off completely and does not help us to believe that Bible Truths are very helpful in solving our burning contemporary issues.

Some modern styles of worship are far more intimate and do try to bring God down to the emotional level of present-day experience. "Just as I am" for instance, or "Near to the Heart of God" or "Beyond the sunset" strike an emotional chord which soothes and comforts. However they still tend to place Deliverance *somewhere else* in space and time (in a nebulous state called "Heaven"). It seems to be overlooked that Jesus' basic instructions bade us work and pray for "Thy Kingdom" to come *"On Earth* as it is in Heaven." Not realizing the basic psychological facts which enable us to work scientifically *on ourselves* to accomplish this Deliverance *here* and *now*, how can the worshipper progress in Spiritual stature?

One of these basic psychological facts is that the breeding ground of our difficulties is *in our subconscious*, (which is formed by our moment by moment choice of conscious thinking and emotions). Another basic fact is the discovery that we *do* have Power of Choice over our thinking and over the principles which we embrace. Without these realizations the maturing Intelligence is all at sea and relegates earthly calamities and frustrations to the Realm of the inscrutable and irrational Will of God.

Thus the confused Individual abandons his basic Purpose on Earth—his responsibility to participate in the age-long battle against earthly limitation. Nothing is then left for him but escape into some futile illusion such as addiction to drink, dope, illegitimate sex or just plain pleasure-seeking. War and crime stories further serve to convince him that the world-error is *elsewhere* than in himself; so that "the other guys" become the scapegoats, and his aim in life turns into a desperate attempt to avoid imminent disaster by imploring the Lord to perform a vicarious, Mystic Act called Salvation—*for him*.

Do we exaggerate? Just study the prevalence of physical, mental and Spiritual collapse in this new generation.

In later life the confused Spiritual concepts and tendency to avoid Spiritual responsibility often linger; and even if we are fortunate enough not to have been bombarded with the hell, fire, and damnation type of teaching, we still live with the impression of a very arbitrary (and pre-Christian) God Who is remote and rather inept and Who, to be honest, does not seem to have His Universe very well under control.

As to the *abstract* nature of God, upon which Christianity was founded, we do not feel that this is sufficiently realized and taught even today. In short, God and the Lord have not been presented in terms acceptable and usable by the 20th century *scientific* mind.

Inadequate as a Spiritual Authority? For the New Age, yes, heartbreakingly so. But when we realize that the Council of Nicaea, which placed Christianity under the Roman Government, was confronted with the task of preserving one Ray of Light from Galilee against a mass of almost global darkness, we become more understanding.

Nascent Christianity had to be put into a protective shell as the hordes of heathen began to be permeated by Its hallowing influence. As a nut is encased by a tough surface to survive the winter, so Christianity was embalmed in a casing of ceremony, parable and imagery to survive the Middle Ages. "To them it is given in parables." That it did survive fills us with admiration for those who fought the great battle of Nicaea and for those who have carried on the work to date. What a wonder that they did permit the tremendous Mystic Truths to come down to us at all!

We marvel and we understand. But that is no excuse for

us to fail in *our* historic task of *de*-shelling the greatest of all Messages and of revealing the sweet, all-nourishing kernel of the nut. The kernel of course is the final Revelation that Mankind is the beloved Son-Daughter of the Most High, and inherits Its Divine Faculties, including the Faculty of inherent Creativity. We create our destinies by the Power of our Thought—both our conscious and *our subconscious* Thought.

This de-shelling is being done today and will continue until that kernel is liberated and made available for *all*. Jesus admonished the astonished Nicodemus (who represents Old Established Authority which thinks it knows it all) "Art thou a Master of Israel and knowest not these things?" And also "You must be born again"—i.e. "You must start all over in your Spiritual thinking and embrace the essential Truths of Reality Which I am demonstrating."

Now we come to our 4th Authority—the Love-Life.

Just about when the child has adjusted himself or herself to the preposterous customs of Earth-life (so very different from those of the Realm from which he came here), comes that most potent pressure of all—the Love-Life.

Since the Love-Life is the guardian of the function of propagation, the Race has taken charge of its activities with a vengeance. This it has a right to do since the fruits thereof will be its future citizens.

We blush to speak of the over-zealous guardianship which has prevailed in some Christian quarters. One misstep from the rigid code of marriage could in certain social circles spell lifelong martyrdom for the lady with only a slight frown directed at the offending gentleman. With all due respect for the beloved Apostle Paul, we deplore his dictum concerning the Spiritual and social inferiority of women. Fortunately, most people no longer accept this aspect of Paul's teaching. But subconscious thought-patterns still mar the balance which is essential if the Race is to use its basic man-woman polarity in the present advanced grade of human Creativity.

We do not find anything at all in Jesus' words or actions to support Paul's prejudice. Jesus said "The man and the woman are One." If One, how can the man be the "head" of the woman? He can't—in the sense in which many people still interpret this passage. Paul himself knew better. For he said "There is neither Jew nor Gentile; there is neither bond nor free; there is neither male nor female."

So our most potent of Earth-forces (the love-life) having in this New Day rejected the Authority of the Middle Ages is trying to find its way alone. What utter confusion results! Not clearly perceiving the four levels of their own Be-ing, most young people do not know whether they are motivated by physical, emotional, mental, or Spiritual urges. At teen-age it is quite likely to be the physical, or at best the emotional, which propels them into the channel of least resistance. Having observed that repression, as practiced by some of our most pious citizens does not always produce the integrated and fulfilled Individuality which we all seek, they try the opposite. Liberated from the check which Mother Nature puts on sexual misbehavior in the form of illegitimate babies, they hail the gift of physical science in the form of pills and other measures which they assume allow freedom without penalty. The penalty comes—and is seen far and wide today in degenerated bodies, malformed babies and psychotic Individuals of all ages.

And as for their having achieved sexual and emotional *fulfillment*, do the majority of our Blessed young people look or act as tho they were experiencing such?

Does our young couple really want this unclean life which is in vogue today, with its grievous results? We doubt it. Perhaps they are merely over-compensating for the extreme repression of the Victorian Age.

The cure, like all cures, is Spiritual. The young people—and older ones also—are floundering towards the *Spiritualization* of that most marvelous of Earth-satisfactions, the love-life. They will make it too. In fact it is possible that the reaction against married rigidity indicates a faint and far-off glimmering of the great Truth which Jesus announced when He said "In the Resurrection they neither marry nor are given in marriage." Impossible as it may seem at present for many people to accept this saying, yet it still gleams as a distant Beacon guiding to a state where we can retain the marvelous cross-current of Love which flows between Man and Woman, yet Spiritualize it to the point where it does not need the old physical outlet as most people have known it but finds its Creative outlet in Spiritual Service to the Race as did Jesus.

This Service we find to be the only perfect sublimation of the sex desire. It frees us from the *voluntary* slavery which we have been under by allowing ourselves to be ridden by the *outer*, superficial aspect of that marvelous Earth-activity—the love-life.

This sublimation eliminates the necessity of confining our Love to one person. The *Spiritualized* exchange between man and woman frees us so that we are in truth, *Universalized* Individuals.

The young couple (or bachelor person) has not gone very far in life before Business, in various aspects, lays its firm hand upon them. Houses must be paid for. Babies need a lot of extras. And in fact, marriage is Nature's favorite way of turning light-hearted, egocentric youngsters into mature, responsible citizens.

Perhaps we might say that the most *personal* aspects of this grim 5th Authority—Business—have been ameliorated. 8-hour days, fringe benefits, compensations of various kinds. The iron grip is far more gentle than ever before in history for the working person.

Or is it? Uncertainty still prevails and results in nervous, reckless attitudes. Medical costs soar. Commuting conditons require huge outlays of time and money. Standards of elegance demand a high tribute. And modern recreations cost fabulous amounts. To say nothing of the steady march of inflation threatening to offset salary gains. And taxes! Say no more. Our point, we are sure, is clear.

In fact that old bogey—fear—has not been laid to rest. People in general feel that something is menacingly wrong.

They visualize an esoteric group of Individuals who manipulate conditions in a way far beyond their own comprehension. And this manipulation they suspect is neither generous nor wise. Bureaucracy still has us, even tho the emphasis has shifted from kings and lords to Big Shots who, it is suspected, still thirst for the blood of the Common Man.

Of course the underlying error is common to both Big Shots and Little Shots. Not the *love* of money but the *worship* of money is the culprit. Business has accomplished marvels. In service, in courtesy, and in all-around responsibility, our business houses are outstanding in history. BUT many people seriously and unashamedly do appear to value money ahead of highest Principle, ahead of freedom, ahead of homemaking, ahead of common sense, and certainly ahead of the practice of *Advanced* Christianity. Money is the *result* of Creative Service given to the Race by each Individual in accordance with the Divine abilities given him or her by her Christ Identity. If he or she is *determined* to give out on this level, regardless of prestige, luxurious conditions, or monetary return, he or she is far better off in the long run and in the meantime has Peace of mind, true Self-Expression, and the chance to enjoy life on his own terms.

It is the character of the people and their willingness to *give* in terms of Service to the All, which projects our earthly prosperity. Underlying materials are inexhaustible as we are now discovering in the form of solar energy, new minerals, deep-sea vegetation, etc. Our essential character is God-like (Outgiving). But thru ignorance and fear we have not yet developed our own Spiritual potential and so have produced short-circuits in our material prosperity as in our bodies and all else.

There is nothing for free in this Universe. We earn what we get either by physical or mental work or by Right-of-Consciousness. A high Consciousness is in Itself a Service if properly used. But still It must *give out* in order to attract Divine Substance sufficient to embody Its mental Creations. Not understanding this, Man has come to believe that he can acquire riches far beyond what he is yet able or willing to earn by Service or by Right-of-Consciousness. His clever *lower* mind leads him to become a speculator instead of a producer; and tho this may *appear* to work superficially *for a time*, it does not pay off in the long run.

Closely allied to Business is our 6th Authority—the Law. Our Law is wonderful. Flexible, impartial, and compassionate to a degree not known before in history for a large nation, it excels in recognizing human values. On the whole our judges have held a high standard of integrity. But our Law is so complicated, what with the ramifications and technicalities of such a diverse Republic, that it is ponderous and rather awesome to the layman. Many citizens hesitate to invoke its expensive services so that it becomes an esoteric luxury rather than a safeguard for the rights of the average citizen. In short, our Law is in part a product of the previous Age and needs revision in the Light of the New Day.

Doctors! The white-robed profession which has been a God-send to Humanity in relieving the sufferings of its immaturity. There have been few sweeter pictures piercing the gloom of past centuries than Florence Nightingale, with the lamp in her hand bringing Compassion to the Hades of the Crimean war-wounded. Her successors, as heralds of the New Age, have distributed their Tender Loving Care ever since. Without regard for their own comfort (or even safety) nurses and their faithful aides have shared the worst conditions of Earth with afflicted mortals; and are doing so today.

But, like other Authorities of the Age just passing, the Medical profession (our 7th Authority) is up against a new situation today. Many patients today prefer to take a pill or a shot, thus passing the responsibility for their cure or their rejuvenation to the doctor, rather than to alter their own horrendous living habits or to do their own Spiritual work. They beg for drugs to keep them "comfortable," not caring that the price of such false comfort may be the deadening of their Higher Faculties and the fostering of addiction which neither they nor the doctors can reverse.

Without placing the blame on any one group for the grotesque picture which exists today, we simply opine that this situation must adapt itself to the New Age. Release from the errors of our materialism can come only from the people—both high and low. We have departed from the knowledge that there is no Power but God, and that the Kingdom of Heaven is *within us*, not primarily on the doctor's shelf. The very word "anti-biotics" should tell the story. "Anti" means "against." "Bio" means "Life." So anti-biotics are against Life. God is Life. So we leave you to imagine what anti-biotics really are. "Fight fire with fire" is the battle cry. "Expel poison with poison." On the contrary, the Bible tells us to *overcome* evil with *Good*.

What is expected of a doctor in our expanding technocracy should not be expected of an Archangel. People fully intend to live longer, better, younger, more happily and more comfortably than ever before. The modern doctor must be an expert psychiatrist, Spiritual advisor, comforter, diplomat and friend, in addition to his stupendous task of keeping up with the preposterous demands of his purely physical science. And practically the whole population consults him regularly, expecting to be cured, psycho-analyzed *and rejuvenated*.

It can't be done from the purely physical angle; and one realizes that the doctor's recourse to prescribing drugs is not necessarily of his own choosing.

We have hopes that Oral Roberts' tremendous project of combining Spiritual and Medical science for physical Healing will introduce a new Era. Instead of a mental ceiling placed by physical science on the present efforts of New Age citizens towards total Regeneration of the body, we now trust that our Heritage of Spiritual-Medical Truth will be given to suffering mortals in New Day terms. This will mean that we can realize *and manifest* the *ceiling-less* objective which our Father-Mother Source now presents to us. World-wide Individual and group efforts for total Regeneration can now (we trust) be coordinated within a framework of Truth which shall make use of both Spiritual and medical techniques.

All down our life journey, unconsciously at first, but more and more consciously as we travel along, we are in the hands of the Social Code, our 8th Authority. "Tell the lady you had a nice time" says Mother to little Annie, regardless of whether or not Annie can say this with sincerity. "Thank you *so much* for the beautiful Christmas present" writes Mrs. Doolittle, who quite possibly gave the beautiful present to the rummage sale. A very nice lady once asked earnestly whether or not it was "all right" to tip up her cereal bowl to scoop out the cream *provided* she tipped it *away* from herself instead of *towards* herself. While worrying about the correct angle for her cereal bowl, this dear lady specialized in unkind personal remarks, to which she apparently felt the social code would have no objection.

The cereal bowl is of course a trivial incident. But the senseless protocol of the social code has exerted its subtle power thruout our whole social and economic structure. For instance, on Wall Street, New York, it was a common saying in the 1920's that advancement depended "Not on *what* you know but on *whom* you know."

There are other tyrannies in our very complex civilization. But we believe we have said enough to present the view that in this New Day conscious Sons and Daughters of the Most High will live from within their own souls with "My Laws written in their *hearts*." When our souls are motivated 24 hours a day by the Christ Consciousness, they will offend no man-made laws but on the contrary will be in harmony with the Universe and therefore will emanate a rich, interesting and purposeful life-picture to the Glory of God and to the assistance and cooperation with all legitimate social agencies.

In the following three short chapters we give a little more attention to three prevalent modern stumbling-blocks—sex, money, and the body (now agonizing under the belief in *outer* remedies rather than in revitalization from Within by Universal Spirit).

UNIVERSAL SPIRIT
(Dimensionless)

The Absolute

Infinite *Un*expressed Being
(Father-Mother God)

↓

Focalizes
Itself
as

↓

Universal Self-Awareness
(The Word, The Universal Christ, The I AM)

↓

The Christ Plane →

Which focalizes
Itself
as the

Individualized Spirit
(Individualized Consciousness)

↙ ↓ ↓ ↘

The Soul Plane →

Here it divides and manifests as two Streams of
Consciousness which interact on the three lower planes in
masculine and feminine aspects (positive and negative)

↙ ↘

Mental Plane

Masculine or
positive
manifestations
on this side
↔

Feminine or
negative
manifestations
on this side
↔

Emotional Plane

Physical Plane

↓ ↓
Man Woman

What we see as a woman on the physical plane started in the *positive* aspect on the Soul Plane, became negative on the Mental Plan, positive again on the Emotional Plane and Negative on the Physical. Vice versa for the man. By exchanging qualities on the Physical Plane, both acquire their opposite faculties and travel back up (in) to Universal Spirit (Consciousness) in full control of all qualities needed for Cosmic Creativity.

CHAPTER 12

Sex

Referring to our diagram on the preceding page we see that the Odic Stream of Life divides on the Soul Plane into two Streams of Consciousness. The interaction between these two seeming opposites projects manifested Form, as the interaction between positive and negative poles of a battery produces the objectified current.

This diagram is based in part on the ancient Wisdom of the Egyptians and/or the Greeks. The Chinese too have long been conscious of the two interacting forces thruout all manifested life. The Chinese call them Yin and Yang and feature them in their art constantly.

In fact all peoples observe this duality which pervades Creation. The Hindus speak of "pairs of opposites;" and it is safe to say that no manifestation is possible without adherence to the Law of Balance, which is really the recognition of these equal but opposing principles.

In architecture we are taught that two principles always exist—the principle of Extension and the principle of Limitation. A library, for instance, must extend a certain distance and must cease to extend, or be limited, at some point. The extension depends upon its particular purpose and the limitation upon the fulfilling of that purpose. As you can see, extension implies limitation and limitation implies extension. Neither can exist without the other.

On the Earth plane, at the Human level, these two opposing principles objectify as Man and Woman. They are One at the level of Universal Spirit and it would seem obvious that they are always seeking to return to that Oneness. It is the tension set up by the interacting of these two Life Streams

(Streams of Consciousness) which projects all outer manifestation. This tension exists only in the *relative* world. In the Reality of Spirit, the Man and the Woman as Jesus said, are One.

It is this tension which makes the man-woman relationship by far the most tantalizing, the most challenging, the sweetest and the most thorny of all our earthly experiences. Spiritually we are seeking what some Metaphysicians call our "mathematical opposite;" and any union less than this is inadequate (incomplete). It is said that for every true soul-union there are now hundreds of karmic marriages; and this is understandable when we consider that Mankind has been trying to live by his physical and emotional urges rather than by his Spiritual Self-hood.

We see from our diagram that these two Life Streams are equal. Seeming differences arise as each Stream emphasizes either the active or the passive aspects of Be-ing in Its Purpose of particularizing certain Principles on the various planes of manifestation.

It is this difference *in emphasis,* coupled with their innate and abiding Oneness which causes the potent attraction between the two. The final resolving of this difference in the perfect union of Spirit, mind, emotions and body, no doubt can give a foretaste of the Bliss Consciousness when experienced within the Awareness of Universal Spirit Which is the Universal Christ.

We do not take as dim a view as most regarding the prevalence of marriage trouble in the modern world. In this New Age it would seem that couples are groping desperately for the higher union of Spirit-Mind rather than that of emotion and body only. Having formed the habit of *lust,* which *takes* rather than of *Love,* which *gives,* the lower impulses still prevail in many cases. Also a deep unbalance has existed since Woman has been considered inferior by many; and there can be no complete harmony on any level on such an erroneous premise.

The greatest motive on Earth is the Giving of Life. When this is done deliberately (consciously) with happy consent on the part of *both* parents, we shall bring in new citizens whose lives have a *Spiritual* foundation. How can we expect to attract a soul with a Life Giving vibration if our coming together is for self-satisfaction rather than for Service to the All? Love gives; and lust grabs. It is as simple as that. And like attracts like in conception as in all else. So our world redemption starts at this point. At which level is our mating—the physical level, the emotional level, the mental level or the Spiritual level? At whatever level we come together, our motivation must be to *give life* at the highest level of consciousness of which we are capable.

Undoubtedly the adjustment of our generative errors will be (and is) horrendous in its social implications. The Cosmic Law is using this, as all other human griefs, as a lever to prod the blundering Race upwards, onwards, into its Spiritual maturity.

Only by such ructions can we tear away our crystallizations and come into the Kingdom of Spirit. And only in the Kingdom of Spirit can the two opposites—Extension and Limitation (activity and passivity)—be harmonized and come to rest.

We know at all events that a very different experience is in store for both man and woman from what they have yet perceived. For Jesus said, "In the Resurrection they neither marry nor are given in marriage but are as the Angels."

CHAPTER 13

Money

"Lord, which is the greatest Commandment of all?"

"The greatest Commandment is 'Hear oh Israel, the Lord thy God is One.'"

God is One. God is Goodness. And God is *All*. When we know that, we have it made.

BUT when the One steps into particularization It *appears* as two opposing forces. "Let US make Man in OUR Image" said God. And so it was. Divine Activity manifesting as opposite to Divine Passivity. Divine Idea manifesting as opposite to Divine Substance. The Masculine Life-Stream as opposite to the Feminine Life-Stream. Man as differentiated from Woman. And so on, down to the very last jot of Creation.

Manifested Be-ing is a Circle. And when the two Life-Streams, interweaving thru the dimensional planes, finally evolve an organism which can perceive its own participation in Universal Oneness, that organism immediately does so and heads back Home into the One-Consciousness. So Mankind in Consciousness rounds the bottom of the Circle and rises upwards from his nadir of purely physical awareness; up thru emotional experience; up thru lower mental activities; thru abstract mind conceptions; until he gains his Purpose and opens himself consciously into the Universal Allness. Here Divinity welcomes him with open arms and flows into him, completing the Circle of Creation. Thus God, particularized in this *Individualized* but open-ended Unit of Christ Consciousness, transcends duality and limitation and expands forever by perceiving and manifesting *new* patterns of Universal Ideas.

It is said that the human brain is developed by the excess sex power which is available to man and woman over and above what is needed for legitimate propagation. This power can flow either up the spine to the brain or downwards into the sex function. The allegory of Adam and Eve relates that Eve and Adam were told not to feed upon (appropriate for their own pleasure) the tree which stood in the midst of their garden (the spine). If they did, they would "surely die." Eating of the fruit of this tree (using the spinal 'seminal' fluid unnecessarily for sense satisfaction) gave them the *relative* concept of Good *and* evil; which is an egocentric concept and which nullified their *Universal* concept of the All-Good, God. In other words their Spiritual nature was starved by the seminal fluid flowing *downwards* instead of upwards to the brain.

Since then, the Race has firmly believed that it must "surely die;" but it resents the implication that this dying, with all its hideous by-products, was only a temporary penalty imposed by a merciful God acting thru Cosmic Law. The Law said that Mankind should be put out of its state of freedom "Lest he put forth his hand and eat of the Tree of Life and live forever." What could be worse than to live forever in the benighted and static condition into which we had plunged ourselves?

Of course the Redemption comes, not thru some vicarious Mystic ceremony but by the mental and Spiritual maturing of each Unit of Christ Awareness into complete self-knowledge *and* self-control.

What has all this to do with Money—our chapter heading? Just this. Money is the outpouring of all-pervading Divine Substance (the counterpart of Divine Idea). It is the manifestation of Divine Love (the counterpart of Divine Truth). It will flow unquestioningly into Divine Ideas, giving Them form so that each Individual Christ Consciousness may see Them, enjoy Them, and pass Them on to younger souls still struggling up the ladder of Self-Awareness.

In other words money is the objectification of the Feminine, Passive, Substance Element of which the Universe is composed; as differentiated from the Masculine, Active, Idea Element of which it is the opposite aspect.

There is no lack of Divine Substance anywhere. We breathe It, eat It, think by It and act by It. But Adam's "curse" or rather his misconception after he misused the seminal fluid (which is a high concentration of Divine Substance), was that he thought he must attract his Substance by his own physical efforts; ("the sweat of his brow"), instead of by conceiving Divine Ideas which would automatically magnetize Divine Substance sufficient for Their fulfillment. Having eaten of the tree of the belief in Good *and* evil, (or the knowledge that he could act separately from the Universal Purpose), he embraced the egocentric viewpoint. His ideas became *self-seeking* and so attracted Universal Substance only with great personal effort.

Henceforth he entertained the false concept that some substances and people were Good (for his own Individual ego) and some were "evil" (disadvantageous to his own personal self-will). Thus the Universe lost (*for him*) Its character of Universal Goodness and Out-Givingness, so that he now thinks he must delve and dig and kill in order to survive.

Rebelling against the drudgery of slaving for his maintenance Man has endeavored to "rise above" it by pressing less mature souls into his service. Dimly perceiving that his salvation would come thru mental development, he strove to raise his consciousness up from purely physical and emotional levels and so developed the *lower* mind, which is very clever at figuring out ways and means of *material* prosperity with self-interest as the motivating force. But in this stage he has not grasped the Divine, or Universal, aspect of Mind so that his results have been spotty to say the least. In other words his motives have been less than Universal and therefore his manifestation is far less than Divine.

Divine Substance allows him to hang himself with his own rope. Consequently an arsenal of atom bombs now stands ready to destroy the Race and a sheet of smog smears the planet with refuse thrown off from his imperfect attempts to live without working (let the machines and the weaker souls do the work). Also he "overcomes" the limitations of space with various conveyances which he has not the maturity to control and which consequently strew the highways with horror. And so on down the dismal list of his attempts to gain his freedom by *egocentric* use of his Divine Powers, operating on Divine Substance by personal will backed by his *lower* mentality.

The "Me First", or egocentric ethic is quite a creditable one in present-day Earth-life. But it is contrary to Cosmic Law. The Great Law says that he who puts himself first shall be last and the last first. He who is greatest among us should wash the feet of the others. And he who helps himself to a high seat at the Feast shall be snubbed by his host and put down lower; while he who seats himself in a lower seat may be invited to come up higher.

Man's aspiration to live without working (in the sense of the mechanical drudgery which now fills his days) is sublime. But his only way of achieving this is by learning to conceive *Divine* (Universal) Ideas *and by implementing Them for the Good of every last Unit of this evolving Cosmos.* This is his natural function and will give him Joy, Freedom and Abundance instead of mental drudgery and neurosis.

The remedy in practical terms for our present dilemma? Very simple. Think *Give* instead of *get*. Instead of panting after money, which unless permeated by Divine Idea becomes a bane rather than a Blessing, simply turn Within and ask the Universal Mind-Love what is Its Purpose for you on this plane at this time. Then *follow same*, regardless of age-old material, emotional, mental or social pressures to the contrary. When you have found your Creative Outlet, (which will be some very interesting Service for the Good of *all*) work yourself into it under your Inner Guidance in an *orderly* way. We are so far off the Beam, most of us, that it may take many years to pay off our karma and be free for Universal Service. But in the meantime we shall be very purposeful and happy provided that we let *God* put a value on our services money-wise instead of telling Him-Her how much we need in order to live according to our own standard, which may contain more than a grain of show-off or of downright *de*structive activity.

If we work for God we *know* that our right compensation will come and that it will increase automatically as the years go by and we become more valuable to the Race. Retirement notwithstanding we shall increase in financial freedom. Also we shall find that *this is really just what we wanted to do all the time.*

Unfortunately Man will not usually step from his old battle-scarred egocentric level to the Spriritual basis until he has suffered enough to realize that he does not know everything. The cup of suffering has now been filled for many however so that millions are becoming aware that there *is* a Better Way. How much better to grasp this thru intelligent perception *now* than to stubbornly play out the gruesome game to its horrendous climax!

Money is the *result* of our ensoulment of Divine Ideas. To work primarily for money shows Spiritual ignorance. If in previous or present lives we have wasted our seminal fluid and so deprived our Higher Mind of its ability to conceive Divine (Universal) Ideas, we must correct this and rebuild our Spiritual stature before we can command that automatic Inflow of Divine Substance to which we are entitled.

No man can serve two masters—God and Mammon. As surely as the sun rises, servers of Mammon (worldly self-interest) will pay back whatever they manage to acquire in other ways than by loving, Universal, out-giving Service to the Race. Those who flatter themselves that they live by brain rather than by brawn must be sure that their ideas are Divine Ideas—i.e. for the benefit of the All. Also they must *serve* their helpers (wash their feet) rather than vice versa.

The Race is young (Cosmically speaking). Whatever it does, it overdoes. Imagination, zeal for life, endurance under difficulties, it has. But—time to grow up now, good People. Stop kidding ourselves that more and more dollars will give Serenity, Joy and Inner Richness. These we must develop within ourselves. That wonderful body of yours lives to express Divine Idea, not for shallow show-off. It is made of Universal, imperishable Substance, not of sickly, degenerating cells. That job must be a Service to Mankind which thrills your very Be-ing because it is an outlet for your special Creative abilities.

No, it is not "the system" which causes our limitations. It is dear old *self*. And the remedy lies in the speedy emergence of our new and victorous *Universal* but *Individualized* Self-hood.

Shakespeare said "This above all, to thine own self be true." Emerson said we must set free "the imprisoned splendor" of ourselves. Realize what you *are* as patterned by the dear Lord Christ in His tremendous Demonstration of the Normal Man. If you realize It, you cannot do otherwise than *be* It. And if you are on the level with God, the money will come for all the *God*-Purposes which you can conceive, ensoul, embody and act upon.

CHAPTER 14

Body

"Mine eyes have seen the glory of the coming of the Lord."

Indeed many of us have seen glimpses of this marvel in our bodies; so our problem now is to have the confidence to recognize these marvels, accept them, evaluate them, and allow them to inspire us to still greater upward efforts.

A Tree of Lights may be seen Inwardly, strung along the nerve cord as it branches thru the human body. The trunk of this tree is the spinal cord and the Lights probably are the twelve great nerve ganglia which, as Charles Fillmore says, are the objectification of the twelve basic Powers or Faculties of Man as he or she manifests on this plane.

The Odic Stream, as It sweeps down from On High to nourish us, can be felt entering the body thru the crown of the head and activating, cleansing and beautifying these Centers. It endeavors to restore balance, harmony and inter-communication among our faculties and will do so if our Spiritual nature is receptive, our mind looking upwards (which is really Inwards), and our body sufficiently at ease to accept this, its daily Bread. It is not only daily; it is hourly; and moment by moment; altho at night, when the ethers are thinner, we can usually get a better realization of this Event and so cooperate better. There is a point at dawn and again at dusk when the etheric tides turn and there is a moment of Stillness. This is known to Mystics as the Naff.

Does this not change our perspective with regard to the arid and wearisome belief that our body inharmonies must be treated from the *outer* world? On the contrary, as Jesus said, whosoever will keep His Word will put himself or herself into a consciously receptive condition so that the Odic Stream Which made the body can sweep into its basic Centers of Power and deal with *all* contingencies. "They shall take up serpents—and if they shall eat any deadly thing it shall not hurt them." But the Promises and other Instructions for our Regeneration must be *used*.

A soap manufacturer and a minister were once standing on the corner talking. Said the soap manufacturer;

"How is it, Reverend, that your Religion has been around for a long time and still many people are very much misguided?"

Just then two little boys came along who had been playing in the mud. Said the minister;

"Well my friend, your *soap* has been around for a long time too—and look at the result."

"Ah but you've got to *use* it" said the soap manufacturer.

Another basic Truth about the body is its simple, but all-potent *polarity*. All Creation is polarity and polarities within polarities. "Wheels within wheels" as Ezekiel said.

The main polarity of the body is between the brain and the solar plexus. The brain, thru the pineal gland, *can* open upwards (Inwards) into Spirit; and to a degree it unconsciously does so in all humans of sufficient Evolvement. Its findings from Spirit, when consciously realized *and accepted*, are passed to the solar plexus, which is the throne of the subconscious. Nerves from the solar plexus then proceed to build these Truths into the whole body. The Truths with which we have been nourishing this great "abdominal brain" have been considerably garbled by our *lower* conscious mind, hampered as it is by what the Race has egocentrically believed these many thousands of years. Consequently results in the body and in the Individual's life-picture are horrendous as seen in the Light of the New Day.

This too Jesus had dealt with in His usual manner of

covering Cosmic Truths in one sentence. "Whoso believes my saying, out of his belly shall flow rivers of living water." Yes, truly, as we allow the Odic Stream to flow thru us, using consciously our God-given polarity between the Higher (abstract) Mind and the solar plexus (subconscious), a tremendous Healing Current exists which not only branches into every nerve center of the body, but flows outwards from the abdomen for the healing of the nations and the gladdening of our entire conscious world.

The solar plexus governs the two tremendous Faculties (or Powers) of Man which have their seat in this region,—the heart and the liver. The heart, as we know, is the center of the Love Faculty. The liver and in fact the whole digestive system, are the seat of the Faculty of Discrimination.

Love, if not balanced by its opposite—Discrimination— defeats its own Purpose. Under the misconception which Adam and Eve fell into by partaking of the belief in Good *and* evil, Love can give Itself to relatively *de*structive (egocentric) as well as *con*structive principles. Therefore *in the relative world,* Love must be balanced by Discrimination and vice versa. John and James in Jesus' group were brothers— John of course representing Love and James Discrimination. Jesus called them "Sons of thunder" because they are so powerful.

We cannot put the Infinite into rigid categories. There are many ways of categorizing the marvels inherent in our unbelievably complex bodies. So we do not wish to be arbitrary in describing here a few of the Truths which we have experienced. The Hindus, for instance, postulate a different pattern of vital body centers; and each Individual will find what is best for him for working purposes.

So for you who are travelling the greatest of all journeys and beginning to experience the greatest of all successes, we only wish to *hint* at the marvels in store for us all. As the old hymn says;

80

> "Eye hath not seen;
> Ear hath not heard.
> Neither hath entered into the heart of Man
> The things which God
> Which God hath prepared
> For them that love Him.
> For them that LOVE Him."

And as the psalmist promises;

> "A thousand shall fall at thy side
> And ten thousand at thy right hand.
> But it shall not come nigh thee "

if thou keep the Faith.

CHAPTER 15

Lucifer

What place does this ubiquitous character have in our racial history and in our present upward efforts?

Well it would seem clear that someone or something or at least some *influence* is doing the scavenger work of the Universe. Scavengers work *against* the Odic Stream of Creativity. Or rather they are entrusted with the task of feeding upon and so removing from this earthly scene the bodies of any weak or ailing members of the Life-Waves which are evolving upon this planet. Objective life is a Circle. The Odic Stream, sweeping down from undifferentiated Be-ing into form, passes the nadir of objectification and circles upwards again into Universal Spirit; thus completing the Purpose of Creation by giving the units of various Life-Waves a chance to gain Individual experience in three dimensions and so to hasten their soul-growth.

Units of the Life-Waves which cannot make the full circle in Continuous *Conscious* Life, are forced to cast off their bodies in midstream. This is at present the case with all units of the lower Life-Waves and with most of the units of the Human Life-Wave.

We can see and appreciate the operations of the scavenger forces as they apply to the lower Life-Waves. Buzzards abound wherever animals are present in their natural state. If they did not, the world would be full of decaying carcasses. Or rather, a lower form of scavenger would take over. For Nature leaves nothing to Chance. In fact there is no such thing as Chance. All is planned Order and perfect Security under Cosmic Law.

A buzzard is not a pleasant object to those of us who are

flowing *with* the Odic Stream with the objective of projecting forms which shall be fit training schools for nascent Sons and Daughters of the Most High. Neither do we relish the billions of microbes which are part of the form-destroying forces. No doubt to a buzzard however, another buzzard is quite attractive. It must be so since they mate and continue century after century. So we see that attraction and repulsion are *relative* concepts.

Consider therefore what would be the state of mind of a forward-striving unit of any Life-Wave if he were demoted thru wilful misdoing to the scavenger lines with the daily duty of destroying outworn manifested forms. Would this not cure him of all destructive tendencies which he had harbored? Would this not be a more sensible punishment than burning forever in a lake of fire?

All seem to agree that Lucifer was a beautiful Angel or Archangel and that he fell into pride, egotism and destructive rebellion, harboring the notion that he was as great as Universal Good and could compete with It in the activity of Creation. He was then cast down and, it is said, is now acting as a scavenger force, culling out the weak ones from the Human Life-Wave. This we can believe; for it fits into our picture of an absolutely perfect Cosmos. All is Good; and even such activities as have been entrusted to Lucifer (if this theory is correct) are still Good and necessary *from the Universal viewpoint.*

"Evil" is a *relative* concept; and does not exist in the Cosmic Consciousness (the Absolute).

The notion of an incarnation of *absolute* evil running lawless in God's Vineyard of growing Seedlings is a prehistoric conception. God is Divine Order (among other things) and we may be sure that errant forces are *used* by His-Her Almighty Wisdom as manure is used in our garden to ferment gases which promote fertility.

So our friend(?) Lucifer is doing us a service; and by his (to us) obnoxious activities he is gaining back his humility preparatory to his reinstatement on the *con*structive side of the Circle of Be-ing. We must admit that he seems to be acting with his usual zeal, brilliance (from his own egocentric viewpoint) and dexterity; giving us our testing in minimal time so that our weaknesses may be culled out and this difficult stage of our Evolvement resolved expeditiously.

The writer has had some experience with the Lucifer type of derangement in the Human Race. As Spiritual Practitioner she has dealt with psychoses which parade in the semblance of that character whom we think of as Lucifer. Seemingly arrogant beyond belief. False, subtle and brilliant (or at least clever), one seems to see in these unfortunate Individuals the pitiful results of their having bowed to these qualities and so come under the domination of Lucifer himself.

Of course these poor souls have another Self. Schizophrenia is the term given by psychologists to the condition in which psychotics have a dual personality. The other personality is modest, sincere, and all that Lucifer is not. And we suspect that Lucifer himself is schizophrenic and will some day return to his beautiful Self-hood, forever done with the qualities he now exhibits.

Jesus spoke to "Satan" as tho he were a person. He also spoke to the demons as tho they had intelligence enough to hear Him and obey Him. They asked if they could go into the swine and He gave them permission. We do not believe that Jesus acknowledged *absolute* evil as embodied in an entity called "Satan." (How could there be *absolute* evil when God is All and God is All-Good?) We prefer to think that Jesus knew the scavenger lines and recognized that they too are a part of the evolving Creation.

It is astonishing how it improves our disposition to be rid of the idea of *absolute* evil. Since evil is now *relative* only, we know we can defeat it by rising into the Consciousness of the All-Good. Also we no longer subconsciously resent God's seeming indifference to our state of siege by a subtle and ruthless Alter-Power. *There is no Power but God (Good),* and we now understand Lucifer's function in our Evolvement and can therefore wage a *good-natured* and fearless battle against his machinations.

We have sometimes wondered why Jesus did not *destroy* the demons—or Lucifer himself for that matter. True, the swine rushed into the sea and were drowned. But we are not told that the demons too were destroyed. In none of Jesus' encounters with the demons do we recall that the demons were obliterated; and we are inclined to believe that this is because they are serving a Purpose in the Circle of the Evolvement of Form. Each incomplete form must be turned back into the etheric reservoir by means of dissolution until the Entity which projected it learns to invigorate it and transmute it forever into higher and higher vehicles for Spirit.

If "evil" were localized in one entity—Satan—would it not have been easier for Jesus to destroy him and his helpers than to convince 6½ billion units of the Human Life-Wave of the necessity of overcoming their own error Individually?

So Jesus' objective was evidently not to destroy the scavengers but to call upon the Christ Identity of each person who was ready and willing to rise above the level where the scavengers could reach him or her. On the physical level these scavengers might take the form of microbes causing disease and death. On the psychic and mental levels they might be demons of various types.

Possibly Lucifer is in charge of all Earth's scavengers so that only by "agreeing with our adversary quickly," or putting Lucifer in his place (behind us) as did Jesus, can we become free to travel the Way of our own Resurrection.

Truly the past *is* behind us; and we must keep it there—not only out of *sight* but out of *consciousness* (including our *sub*conscious). It does not exist for us except as a former training ground for the development of our inborn Spiritual qualities which are establishing our Christ Identity in complete Spiritual freedom.

Use our Spiritual Power for physical necessities (make bread out of stones)? For show-off (leap from the Temple)? Or for dominion over others (rule the nations)? No thank you Mr. Lucifer, we are no longer even *interested*. Get thou behind us *forever*. These things belong to our *past*, not to our radiant, life-giving Future.

In fact, Mr. Lucifer, in the vibrant words of our younger generation, we "couldn't care less" for your suggestions. To be honest, Mr. Lucifer, you and all your doings "turn us off" *completely*.

CHAPTER 16

One Neurotic Rat

A bright young rat once fell into the hands of a psychology research worker who wished to study mental unbalance.

The unsuspecting rat was starved until all his faculties were focussed urgently on *food*. He was then loosed into a corridor at the end of which were several cubbyholes with swinging doors at a slight elevation from the floor. The odor of cheese prevailed.

The rat rushed down the corridor and jumped at one swinging door. No cheese. He tried another. No cheese but still that tantalizing smell. Finally he located cheese—in the second cubbyhole from the left end.

Next day the same procedure and Mr. Rat remembered his former success and jumped at the second door from the left. No cheese. He jumped at a few more doors and located cheese in the third door from the right end. The third day he jumped a little wildly but finally was successful. Still his little mind held firm, remembering former successes and intelligently persevering.

The fourth day—ah what a mean God must be up there in the blue! No cheese in any cubbyhole, but still that haunting smell and still that dire necessity of finding something to eat. He tried the doors which he had successfully tried before. Tried them all again at haphazard as reason began to give way to emotion. No cheese. Tried them all again and then kept on jumping wildly without reason until his strength was exhausted.

From then on he was one neurotic rat. He crouched in a corner, trembling with frustration. When a bit of strength returned he would dash madly round and round without plan or reason—anything to have the feeling of "doing something." Faith and self-confidence had given way to impassioned, physical action, ungoverned by mind. In this condition it is doubtful if he would have recognized the cheese if he had stumbled over it.

Have you seen it in the Human species? Too much frustration wrecks the conscious control so that lower urges take over and the original purpose is lost in a blur of resentment and fear.

In the rat's case, his loss of Faith was justified. For there *was* a superior mind deliberately trying to confuse him. He was purposely given more to handle mentally and emotionally than his limited brain and nervous system could cope with. But in the Human case, our Parent-Intelligence does no such thing to us. Our Father-Mother is Intelligence-Love working at the *Universal* level; and It does not make sport of Its creatures by posing riddles without answers. However, by the Laws of Be-ing, we are placed in such a way that if we persist in our egocentric purposes contrary to Universal ones, we find ourselves in a bind as did the *innocent* rat. This is necessary in order for us to develop the Higher Spiritual Comprehension which forms our Individual Christ Identity. It is time for us to develop our Creative Faculty and to open that *upwards* into *Universal* All-Goodness.

If we refuse Enlightenment, we keep jumping at objectives which we assume will bring us joy, fulfillment and soul-satisfaction but which do not in the long run. At every step in each Individual's Evolvement he or she *has the chance* to listen to the Higher (Inner) Voice Which tells him he is wrong when he exhibits egocentricity below what is expected of him at his Evolutionary age. If we laugh it off when "conscience" or some more mature Intelligence warns us, we start on the unreasoning emotional path which brought Mr. Rat to utter irresponsibility.

As in Jesus' case (the three Temptations), Lucifer, Satan, or whatever you may call it (him) will always be on hand to test a Christed Individual. By his insinuations and flatteries he culls out our weaknesses (pride, greed, fear, sensuality, power-lust etc). For the Christed Consciousness must be strong enough to stand *alone* against all possible human illusions. It must arrive at the point where "none of these things move me"—not the howling bluff of fear, nor the flattering urge of personal ambition, nor the simpering whisper of sentimentality. And last of all, not the hypnotic down-drag of absolute nothingness which is called "death." "The last enemy which shall be overcome is death."

Man being infinitely complex, he accumulates as the ages pass many incarnations' bitter fruits which cause tangles in his subconscious and which objectify in events which may seem to him the arrangements of a mean and inscrutable Deity. He does not realize that our infinitely merciful Parent-Source has warned us, told us, implored us, inspired, and almost begged us to *listen* to the Inner signs and so to avoid the dire results of egocentric action. While riding high the average immature human reasons backwards. His outward flashes of "Success" convince him that he has outwitted the Cosmic Law. When the crash comes he is totally nonplussed and takes preposterous measures to evade the whisperings of his lordly mind which is still reiterating the deep Truths which he is unwilling to accept.

A tragic condition indeed. And how similar to that of the neurotic rat! However everything that happens in this Cosmos has a Purpose; and when Mr. Man *acknowledges* himself to be at the end of his own rope, he still has one option—to turn his lordly mind *upwards* and enlist his *Spiritual* Faculty. As age-old tragedies were instantly healed by Jesus Christ Who is One with our Father-Mother Source, so God-Universal can and will immediately flash the Light of Truth into our tangled brain when it is at last willing to admit "there cometh One mightier than I."

The cup of earthly entanglement is now about as full as Man's *lower* understanding can contain. In fact millions of highly evolved Individuals have given over reason and are driven by wild emotion into blind channels which they are powerless to reverse, such as drink, dope, suicide etc. "Be ye not troubled" said Jesus "For these things must needs be." Man as a whole must come to the state where he *knows* he is at the end of his own rope before he will give up trying to beat the Cosmic Law, and turn in joy and confidence *and humility* to his Maker for the Divine Fulfillment which is just what he has been seeking in all his grotesque bedevilment.

P.S. We note that the sufferings of the neurotic rat served a purpose far greater than he could possibly imagine. So do ours also. And for *all* there is Comfort and Compensation in this perfectly balanced Cosmos in the ratio of at least 1000 to 1.

P.S. The account which we read of the neurotic rat did not say whether or not he recovered from his breakdown. But psychiatrists tell us that when a Human Being *overcomes* such a condition he or she is not only normal as before but has arrived at a *super*-normal development.

CHAPTER 17

Sea of Glass? We Think Not

Now that we have resolved (in imagination at least) most of our worst personal and racial difficulties, we should like, if the reader pleases to turn our thoughts *forwards* to the joyous prospect of what we hope to experience as we advance on the golden path of Self-Awareness, or Regeneration.

Our Imagination is one of our twelve basic God-Faculties. When Jesus welcomed Nathaniel (who stands for Imagination) to His Inner Circle, He said "Behold an Israelite indeed in whom is no guile." The term "Israel" was the name given to Jacob after his struggle with the Angel. So it stands for the victorious Regeneration; and we know that those who are Spiritually entering into the New Day have indeed struggled with the Angel and so deserve to be called Israelites,—not of course in a racial sense but in a Spiritual one.

In practical terms our imagination must learn to argue always from Divinely perfect premises instead of from a belief in potential wrongness (evil). For instance, suppose we must cross a busy highway on foot. As we see cars and trucks whizzing in every direction does a sense of fear and confusion dim our perspective as we imagine the disaster which would follow if we or someone else should make a false move? This is Imagination working from a false premise. The Cosmic Mind is perfect. We and all other Units of this Mind are harmonious within that Truth. We all know the traffic laws and obey them meticulously. We hear otherwise; and have seen accidents; and can imagine ourself involved in one. This is an imperfect premise. Accidents do not *have to* occur. For Man has the option of *always* appealing to the Perfect Consciousness so that his mind is made infallible for the purpose in hand.

We may do that; but *others* may not? This is provided for by our all-seeing Parent. In our immature state (while we are learning to use our free-will *correctly*), we are directed to request *constantly* "deliver us from evil." This calls into our Service the armies of Angelic Guardians and Protectors Who are waiting to serve us but Who cannot reach us unless we give our Imagination *Divine* premises to work from. These premises include the Perfection of Cosmic Law *and* of Cosmic *Mercy* (Love). "He shall give His Angels charge over thee to keep thee in all thy ways. They shall bear thee up in their hands lest thou dash thy foot against a stone." We must establish this Truth in our entire subconscious thru our privilege of *constant* Spiritual Communion. (And of course we must keep our attention on the Divine project we have in hand, not wool-gathering concerning possible disaster.)

This practice is "walking with God" which is the main attribute of all great characters in all the annals of history.

So in an endeavor to use our Imagination *constructively*—looking *forwards* into the vista of the All-Good which we are learning to manifest, what do we imagine we shall experience as the New Day dawns, the Kingdom comes, or the Christ Consciousness prevails in us?

This is somewhat like asking "What is Heaven like?" Impossible to answer since there are as many Heavens as there are units in the Life-Wave. Yet there is common ground in our Regenerated experience, so that those who have overcome separateness can harmonize and live in the joy of *mutual* Self-Awareness, which is the Purpose of Creation.

In fact this is our first requirement for the Regenerated Consciousness—a condition of conscious harmonization with others who are enjoying similar ecstasy. At some stages our journey thru the wilderness has seemed a lonely one. But human companionship is our birthright; and the Higher Companionship dawns upon us at a very early stage of our Awakening. It increases as we travel upwards and, we have no doubt, comes into complete fullness in that Kingdom which shall have no end.

Of course the Higher Companionship implies a condition of mutual respect and equality. No bosses allowed nor needed. Coordinators there will be,—experts in this or that area of endeavor. These will be respected by everyone and consulted as to technicalities of a situation. But as for one illumined Individual "bossing" another, that notion is abhorrent to the New Day.

Peace of Mind of course is taken for granted in the New Age. Tensions there must be in any purposeful life. And the Kingdom is full of purposeful people. But tension is not necessarily *worry*. And it is not necessarily unpleasant. If one has a pleasant project in mind, the tension of its prospect is very pleasing; its fulfillment is exciting; and our reward in terms of soul-satisfaction is everlasting. The requirements for this celestial state of mind are (1) we shall *know* that we are capable of doing our chosen job well and without furor or accident; and (2) we shall be able to relax *completely* after it has been launched on its way into eternity. In fact the relaxation (rest) is deeper after each such adventure because, having exercised our Divine Faculties as they were meant to be exercised, they are deepened and enabled to drink ever more freely of the Elysian Springs. Hurry of course is taboo in the Kingdom. As Emmet Fox said "You're going to live forever; so why hurry?"

So we have Spiritual Companionship, purposeful Creative activity, and Peace (Serenity) in our Kingdom.

Freedom of course is taken for granted. Freedom from that old petulent self which kept us striving in the wrong directions and trying to hold onto things which belonged to the past and which perhaps never did belong to us in the first place. This freedom applies particularly to *people*. This seems to us the Principle behind the great fact that no marriage exists in the Resurrection. No one belongs exclusively to anyone. Yet all belong to all. Therefore wherever there is an affinity, it can be used to the full, and appropriate fruit brought forth from the association. The social code will not be nudging us with a guilt complex if we enjoy the wonderful cross-vibration of association with a person of the opposite sex persuasion. We know that marital rigidity was a necessary discipline in our immature *material* consciousness. But freedom unlimited will now be ours; and domination (possessiveness) will be—praise God—a thing of the past. The Spiritual-mental consciousness will now be our usual habitat rather than the physical-emotional.

Music! We are *made* of Music. It is our background, our joy, our relaxation; and one of our Creative outlets. We opine that in our Regenerated state we shall not have to *learn* pieces or songs. Anything that one Regenerated Person knows will be immediately available to all mentally, and can come into consciousness from deep Within as some of us wake up in the morning with a song singing itself in our heart without any conscious reason for its being there. Voices will not have to be "placed." They will come forth like that of the meadow lark,—our natural impulse to Praise and to the Joy of Living.

Similarly with color. Artists will be in their glory. For the Astral Plane is made of color; and new colors can be imagined and brought into consciousness for the enjoyment of all.

Books! Yes, no doubt there are books written in the ethers. Perhaps they are in the form of moving picture stories if we wish to read up on any phase of history or of technical information. The Akashic Records contain impressions of all that has ever happened on Earth—great or small, personal or racial.

Group Worship! We hesitate to put into words our idea of what group Worship must be where all hearts and minds are *fully* dedicated to the All-Good and tuned upwards to absorb still more and more and more of the Infinite Glory as It pertains to Man. The Universal Christ will be a still more dynamic and intimate Presence and our souls will be able more and more to perceive and respond to the practical Inspiration which is ours for the taking.

Bodies! Rest assured, they will be a joy and not a problem

to the liberated Spirit. Whenever limitation is felt we shall know exactly how to turn Within to raise our Consciousness above that limitation forever. Our body will be seen to be a *means to an end* (Purpose), not an end in itself. Therefore its satisfactions will be enjoyable but not paramount in our lives.

In short life will be (and now is, to a degree with some of us) a kaleidoscope of infinitely varied adventure, with our own Christ Identity in control so that no fear of error or limitation or failure can block our progress into still higher and higher states of Awareness.

As you see, our conception of the New Day is a far far cry from the harping Angel and Sea of Glass conception. Angels there will be—and already are—in our midst. But They are Friends, not just Ornaments. And Their marvelous Music is not Their only function. Since our New Day can be on Earth as well as on the next (or Astral) Plane, we encourage people to feel and know the Presence of these glorious Beings as of *here* and *now*; for They are our natural Friends and Guardians. And always—but always—there is Their spontaneous chorale of Healing and of Praise.

We shall give separate chapters to the consideration of what form the ideas of locomotion, economics and hospital-ization will take in the New Consciousness. Even a dim flight of fancy in this direction will show us that our present civilization,—so dominated by the automobile, the stock market and the operating room, will be obliged to undergo enormous changes.

> Thy Kingdom? And what is Thy Kingdom?
> Thy Kingdom is already known.
> Thy Kingdom, my Lord and my Savior
> Is the Birth of one Soul to Its own.

CHAPTER 18

Locomotion

How will it be in the Higher Consciousness—that locomotion which is so necessary in our space-time dimensional world?

Our first thought is that if Mankind had given as much time and effort to conscious *Spiritual* development as he has to manufacturing vehicles to overcome the space limitation, there would be no problem. We could do as we are told they do in the Higher dimensions—simply *think* ourselves to where we want to be.

We suspect, however, that fussy little Mankind in his immaturity, *likes* to exhibit his prowess in the outer manipulation of *things*, regardless of the slavery of inventing and implementing and maintaining these palliatives; and heedless of the imperfections inherent in all mechanisms which are constructed from *without* instead of from *Within*.

Yes, the outer personality enjoys the sense of physical power which throbs under his hand on the steering wheel. He does not see his contraption as a little tin box into which he must wedge himself in order to command that power which he solemnly declares is necessary for the "earning of his living." Adorned as the tin box may be with streamlined proportions, pleasing gadgets, and colors, for the benefit of his admirers, it is still true that the little tin box frequently spills him on the highway in pieces and at best spews out a noxious exhaust which is polluting the atmosphere of the planet.

We do not wish to belittle this partial success which Mankind has achieved in his rebellion against limitation. But as usual, we contend that our gadgets tend to control *us* instead of vice versa. If Man had taken the trouble to really become the "Captain of his own soul," he would be sitting in a much more comfortable seat (metaphorically speaking) and would find the going *much* less dangerous and less expensive.

There is a better way. Starting from *Within*, we can discover it. Perhaps to the mechanical-minded it may seem less glamorous. Perhaps to the profit-seeker it may not wring billions annually from the gullible public. But to us it seems much *more* glamorous; and we note that the excess profit-seeker usually rides a crest and then experiences what is known as the "economic cycle." This cycle is in reality merely the backwash of materialism and greed.

The writer sometimes experiences a much more exhilarating mode of travel in her sleep. Frequently she passes from one place to another (one state of consciousness to another) by a simple method, similar to walking but without its limitations. Instead of a hurried and frustrated sense of battling against the inertness of Mother-Earth, she simply passes swiftly and pleasantly along an aerial pathway in an upright position but without the limitation of successive steps. She notes that no one and no thing ever stands in her way; and she assumes that this is an expression of Divine Order which decrees that there is no conflict of interest in the Consciousness where all is subjected to Universal Purpose.

Of course this is only an elementary stage of Spiritual Transportation. She has also experienced (in sleep) a voluntary rising above the heads of companions. This is a very pleasurable sensation and completely natural. It is the perfect response of our vehicle to our desire to be somewhere else than where we are. No sense of danger accompanies it. No doubt this is the beginning of thought-travel, which some members of the Race are said to have developed to a very usable stage.

We do not consider our experience the same as "Astral journeying" in which it is said that the emotional and mental bodies are forcibly separated from the dense body. The rule for most of the Race at our stage of Evolvement is "Take your dense (physical) body with you wherever you go," except as other experiences may come to us *naturally* in sleep.

If and when we do arrive naturally at Spiritual Transportation, how can we carry our trailer with us? Well in the first place, a person who is able to live in this Consciousness does not need many gadgets. In the second place it is not unreasonable to imagine that such gadgets as are needed can be dematerialized in one spot and reassembled on a higher vibration by thought-power. Our streets will then be free from the endless grumble of cement-mixers, mobile houses, steam-rollers and tons of groceries which now hurtle past our doors. Do we believe in Christian promises? "You shall say to this mountain, 'Be thou removed and planted in the midst of the sea' and it shall obey you." Atoms are Intelligences; and the Higher Intelligence of *mature Man* (the Christ) can speak to them and be obeyed without the agency of derricks or cement mixers.

Nothing at all is unreasonable to imagine if we subject our Imaginations to Universal Purpose and follow it with humility and balance,—desiring marvels only in due order when our characters have developed to the point where we shall use them wisely. At that stage we shall not need the limitations which are safeguards for the immature consciousness lest it injure itself severely in its dash for expediency.

Knowledge of the Odic Stream of Power which comes from Within was presented to Jesus at His Baptism at the river Jordan. Thereafter He was immediately driven by the Spirit into the wilderness, where the race pressures of self-interest assailed Him as He contemplated the use of His abilities.

The first suggestion of "Satan," "mortal mind," "self-interest" or whatever we may wish to call it, was to use the Power for His own nourishment. He was hungry after His long fast and self-interest said "You can make bread out of these stones." This He refused; and presently the Angels came and ministered to Him. The second Temptation was for show-off; "You can astonish everybody by leaping from the roof of the Temple." This He also refused. Thirdly "You can control all the people of the world by Mind-Power." This is to many people a stickler. "How much good I could do if I exercised Power over other people and forced my will upon them!" At this suggestion Jesus saw for all time the complete falsity of what His subconscious was suggesting thru the agency of "Satan" whom we think of as Lucifer. He told the Voice to get behind Him for good; and took the humble, compassionate, narrow way to accomplish His World-Cleansing.

Can we do the same? We shall have to discard a lot of our luxury gadgets, our show-off gadgets, *and* we shall have to shun forever that tendency to use our new-found strength to override a weaker soul's consciousness. Not the slightest hint of domination must ever dim the Jesus Christ Demonstration of calling up and *setting free* the Christ Identity of each person rather than of controlling him or her either materially, emotionaly, mentally or Spiritually by our "superior" development.

This enlightened policy of "considering others as ourself" (instead of "getting ahead" and making use of their gullible condition) will, among other things, prevent unnatural growth in our production facilities. These now tend to "use" weaker souls in an assembly-line manner, thus stifling their Creative development and so keeping them out of the Kingdom.

CHAPTER 19

Economics

How will the great god Business fare in the New Age?

A neighbor of ours once had a dream. A friend of his had just passed and the neighbor was seeking Him in the after-world. The neighbor travelled down a long corridor in which he observed nothing—just nothing at all. Finally he found his friend, a former active business man on Earth, sitting amidst just nothing. "Don't come *here*" said his friend. "There is nothing—but *nothing* here."

Whether or not this denotes actual fact, we believe that the moral is sound. On the next plane, we are told, there is no such thing as business. Consequently those who have given over their whole Being to commercialism as such— i.e. with the money motive predominating,—may find themselves surrounded and immersed in just exactly nothing. For they planted no enduring seeds in their Earth-Life of anything eternally uplifting to the Race.

This is not true of *all* commercialism. As the Middle Ages broke up commerce was a major constructive factor in dissolving the crystallizations of feudalism. As men and women dared the high seas and made paths around the world, peoples became aware of each other from East to West and learned the advantages of mutual communication. *Legitimate* commerce is an integral part of our three-dimensional civilization, and it still bears rich fruit in stimulating understanding between humans.

But as always aggressive expansion must be curbed and softened by the balancing principle of assimilation. Activities which are oriented solely for "Me First" (or the dollar first) can become monsters of egocentricity, which unbalance the economy over the whole planet.

Jesus put His seal of approval on *legitimate* commerce in the parable of the man who was given 10 talents by his landlord and who put them to work so that they increased 100%. We note however that the man did this *for the Manager* (who represents the over-all Intelligence), not for dear old self. Therefore his reward came to him (with a bonus) without his having to demand it. Also he was invited to "enter into the joy of his Lord."

True, this is the Age of Individualism. We are no longer cogs in wheels. But the Truth is that we being Sons and Daughters of the Most High, our greatest self-fulfillment is inseparable from the *Universal* Good. So that only by serving the All in our own Creative way can we find real joy and advancement in life. We can trust Universal Be-ing to *enhance* our Individuality, not to smother It. So we can cooperate with It fully without fear of belittlement.

As a movement decays, scavengers are enabled to destroy it; and as in pirate days, scavenger forces are today challenging that part of our economic activities which are based on pure egocentricity. It is time for the era of *material* expansion to be balanced by the gentler assimilating forces; and for both principles to blend into the Principle of the Whole. As material frontiers wane, *Spiritual* frontiers challenge us in no uncertain terms.

In a spirit of self-correction therefore, let us analyze our wonderful financial system a bit and see where and how we have so far come short of bringing it to its perfect fulfillment of peace and plenty for *all*.

Money is really credit. If a farmer trades a mule for a wheelbarrow with his neighbor, they are exchanging *tangible* assets. But if you run up an electric bill you are living on credit, which means that the electric company believes you will pay at the end of the month. When you pay you give them dollars underwritten by Uncle Sam or John Bull or whatever; which means that the world in general believes Uncle Sam will pay on demand. Fluctuations in the value of the dollar reflect the world's faith in Uncle Sam's financial situation. What will he pay with? Gold? He doesn't have that much. So it is *credit* that the world business really runs on—or the *belief* that a person or a nation has either tangible assets or the ability to give service; and that he will give them on demand.

Did missionaries dealing with the early American Indians carry dollar bills? They carried beads or other gadgets which were the Indians' idea of worthwhile tangible assets. They did not care for intangibles. But money in our present very complex financial set-up may mean a set of figures in a book or it may mean a credit company's idea of what your character and reputation entitle you to. This is a marvelous achievement for the world—to live on faith rather than on barter. It is the basis of our world-wide communication. With a few credentials you can now write a check almost anywhere for what you need.

BUT the credit system can be misused. A certain financial tycoon in the 1920's valued himself *very* highly. Perhaps he had been reading success books which bade him "think positive" concerning himself. He "pyramidded" his assets and talked so big and so convincingly that reputable New York bankers went along with his fantastic operations. They went down with him, too. And so did several million smaller fry. One dark night he found himself penniless and millions of dollars in debt. By morning he was in the next world, shot by his own hand since he could not face the catastrophic results of his "positive thinking."

He (and millions like him) had valued himself *too* highly, and had convinced others of his false reasoning. But he had not convinced *God*. The Cosmic Law is based on sheer *Spiritual* worth; and when we inflate ourselves beyond that point, there comes a day of reckoning. This day is merely a Clearance however. If we alter our ideas and face the fact that in *Spirit* we are worth any amount we can possibly imagine *but* that we must *prove* this by Universal Service in Earth terms (and on *God*'s ledger, not ours), then all is well and we come out happier *and richer* men and women.

"There is nothing secret that it shall not be made plain." So let us be sure that the value we put upon ourselves corresponds with *God*'s Ideas, or our egotism will be made plain and we shall find we have wasted a lot of time and effort trying to arrive at our dreams by will-power instead of cooperating with Cosmic Law.

These Principles apply to Big Shots, Little Shots and Middle-Sized Shots.

In practical terms we have a few comments to make as the forces of assimilation begin their work of harmonization.

We take no stock in the dictum that we must constantly increase the number and complexity of the gadgets which the present generation finds necessary to its prosperity. Reducing them would break the backbone of Society and put people out of work? So runs the battle cry. Is it seriously proposed that there is not enough potential work in the world? And that ever-increasing *material* luxury is the only way of keeping our commercial joy-ride on its upward spiral? Some may say that other occupations do not increase the Gross National Product as does Big Business. But consider how much some of them can *decrease* the Gross National *Outgo*. For instance, all activities which improve the physical, mental or Spiritual calibre of the people greatly reduce the backbreaking load of government expense in caring for deficient Individuals.

No, we cannot believe that material commercialism is the *only* profitable outlet for our Creative energies. Creative outlets are myriad; and we have young citizens capable of initiating new and still more inspirational channels of endeavor. The unbalance lies in the values which the public puts upon material as compared with cultural or Spiritual pursuits.

Our personal income reflects the value which the Race puts upon our services on Earth. At present the monetary reward of the business tycoon as compared with that of the nurses' aide (who daily spends her soul-force combatting the worst filth and fears of Earth) is preposterous. Yet it reflects the valuation which the average citizen puts upon these two occupations. Likewise professional ball players live like kings while our teachers of the young may struggle in garrets. What will the public pay for? Look around you and observe.

But this is only one side of the story.

The public errs in its evaluation of human services. But Creative Individuals often err in not having the courage to develop and present their product so that it can help the Race as a whole in a worthwhile way (for uplift).

So errors in "the system" often boil down to errors in the Spiritual integrity of the citizens—high and low.

We come to Earth to learn a lesson. Being Spiritual Beings we must learn to *implement* our Spiritual natures and truly Creative Ideas in three dimensions and in terms both beneficial and acceptable to the Race at its present state of Evolvement. We must learn the language of the world and make our Gift to Life acceptable to as many as desire it.

Many of our highly evolved Earth-Beings cannot make their abilities felt in Earth terms because they will not come down from the heights and stand on their own special talent to ray out supernal Truth so that It will reach the grass roots. They much prefer to serve the material industries rather than to fight the battle necessary to convince the Race of the value of their Spiritual (Inspirational) product. In other words they "can't afford to be themselves." This results in over-crowding of the material work-force and a great dirth of pioneers in other Creative fields.

The rich young ruler turned away *sadly* because Jesus told him that following his highest Inspiration would require the sacrifice of his material treasure. He *sadly* chose to remain on his old level. Obviously he knew better.

These facts are an integral part of our economic picture. For if even a fraction of our Creative citizens would ply their highest Inner Calling instead of serving the bank account, many of our economic ills would evaporate.

In short, while appreciating what our marvelous techniques and matchless organization have done for us, we submit that there is a fly in the ointment of our out-sized industrialism, and that only by sincere and *constant* reference to the Universal Life, Truth, Love which is the Law of our Be-ing, can this fly be eradicated. As of old, the fly is the worship of "other gods" instead of Principle; of material luxuries instead of Spiritual Advancement; of self-interest instead of Universal Service.

Commercial ethics are a sweet dream compared with what they *used to be*? Ah yes. But are they sweet enough for the New Age? For the Day which is to be, we feel that the quality of Earth-life must be—and shall be—vastly improved *from the inside out*.

On the plus side of the world's economic picture we have already mentioned the great boon of improved working conditions which prevail in many countries. This is a God-sent advance. Another great achievement is such developments as what we call Social Security in the U.S.A. That Senior Citizens are on the way to becoming independent, self-respecting economic units is one very great advantage to the world. Those who have leisure and experience to do their own Creative thinking are becoming a great Inspirational influence. And the dreaded "economic cycle" is now cushioned by the buying power of millions who are assured of this basic income and will buy rock-bottom necessities regardless of inflation and/or depression.

Let us rejoice therefore. Cast off old taboos and regimentations, and believe Truths which are far beyond our present comprehension. They are knocking at our doors; and only by the inspired opening of our consciousness in *all* directions can we let Them in with sufficient Power for us to be able to use Them *Specifically and Universally*.

The Second Coming of the Christ Consciousness depends in part on YOU.

CHAPTER 20

Rest Homes

Will there be any of us in the New Day who will have
lost (temporarily) the ability to marshal our physical and
mental forces into a going concern capable of coping with the
demanding vibrations of Earth?

Ah yes, imperfection will still be with us to a degree, tho
not in the lurid forms which glower at us today from many
directions. Yes, there must surely be havens where therapy
is administered and where, in an even higher octave than
now, white-robed humans will minister to our frailty.

Some rest homes and hospitals today hint at the calibre of
Help which will be given in the coming Earth-Era—our next
way-station on our journey to the Kingdom of Heaven. However the prevailing spirit will then be comparatively devoid of
fear and of horror and of *prolonged* physical disability. We
shall *know* we are on our way upwards, not downwards. And
if some are ready to end their days on Earth but have not
yet learned to go out the *front* door (by voluntary Ascension)
rather than the back door of involuntary dismissal, they will
be lovingly prepared for their next life-chapter (as they are
now), and speeded on their way with happy confidence so
that the Event will take on a festive rather than a defeatist tone.

Indeed we have often visualized what a rest home could
and should be like if its occupants believed (thru their whole
subconscious) even *half* of the glories which they pray and
sing about. If a person has done his or her best in following
what she knows of the Christ Message, will she not "Stand
on the Promises" as the old hymn advises? If she does, then
surely the prospect of laying down the responsibilities of
Earth-life will beckon with shining arms; and the rest home

will become a Graduation Party rather than a house of misery
and frustration, not to say of stark, unreasoning fear.

Alice-in-Wonderland, we are told, is a text-book on Metaphysics. We remember that the Red Queen told Alice "We
serve jam every *other* day—jam yesterday and jam tomorrow;
but never jam today." So it would seem that some Senior
Citizens live mostly in their own emotional yesterdays and
somewhat in the nebulous hope of a Heavenly tomorrow;
but seldom in the joy of today. Could they but grasp the
timeless Truths, they would turn hope into present *knowledge*
and nostalgia for yesterday's emotional triumphs into the
eternal soul-satisfaction which is ours today if we will take it.
Never has a generation had such a chance to use both its
material and Spiritual achievements for the gathering of a
golden harvest in our leisure years preparatory to a still
greater field of enjoyment in our next chapter of endeavor.

We also opine that the companionship of their own
contemporaries in a beautiful spot with outdoor recreation
facilities is the natural environment for those who need
physical and mental rest. New Age citizens do not need to
lean upon their families. They can continue their independent
lives among friends who have similar problems and interests
to their own. And as for a field for human Service! A rest
home provides that for all who are able, so that no out-giving
person could possibly be bored.

We see the beginnings of this happy prospect today. In
each hospital or retirement home there are a few who take the
enlightened view of their present situation. What an opportunity these few have of raying out the Truth in human,
everyday terms which are acceptable to the many who feel
that this is the way things ought to be but are not in the
average present consciousness!

Two freedoms are necessary before the spirit of our healing facilities will fully reflect the Way of the Lord. These are
(1) freedom from over-zealous family attachments centering
around the *past*; and (2) freedom from the fear which comes

as a result of leaning on purely physical means of healing. (This includes the urgent need of freedom from habitual drugging.) A person who wishes to graduate into New Age concepts can use and appreciate much of what has been formulated thru the centuries by physical healing ministries. But he or she need not be *dominated* by them if so be that she has turned Within and submitted *all* levels of her consciousness to the Enlightenment received from Inner Communion.

Of course New Age Healing will emphasize measures taken to align and purify the *Inner* bodies as well as the outer dense body. Such measures have been known to a degree for many centuries and are known today in scattered areas. Most doctors today value psychological considerations and try to relieve emotional tie-ups. Natural diet and elimination of drugs are understood by many. Some health agencies give music therapy and colored light treatments. Spiritual groups reach for (and sometimes attain) purely Spiritual Healings.

So in this New Age we are bordering upon (and must grasp decisively if our civilization is to continue) our Heritage of Spiritual, mental, emotional and physical Regeneration. For the nightmare of illness, accident, old-age and lingering death is becoming a monster and will disrupt our economy, undermine our self-confidence, and reverse our Faith if we do not live up to the Highest that we know.

In short, beginning *now* we must have havens where Spiritual and semi-Spiritual values are paramount. Why should not the great and various groups of Healing collaborate to drive out this demon of fear and of the acceptance of inevitable disease and death? Why should not *preventive* therapy be our first concern? It can and must be done pretty soon—or else.

Part III

CHAPTER 21

Personal Saga

Now if the reader pleases we should like to trace a few of the steps by which this unit of potential Christ Consciousness has arrived at the threshold of the New Age. Her life so far has been remarkably varied and interesting in that many many groups and Individuals have formed the pattern of her days, so that she feels she has taken the pulse of this generation with all (or almost all) of its extremely dramatic endeavors, difficulties, aims, errors and triumphs.

Born in the old city of Albany, capital of New York State, U.S.A., she did not coalesce in the least with the political-social spirit which was her mother's idea of a very blessed privilege.

Glad to remove to Syracuse, New York, after her father's passing, she there observed—and enjoyed—the life of good American citizens without undue social pretensions. She was able to "be herself" to a large extent, in spite of her mother's great grief and utter bewilderment at life in general and her own destiny in particular. In spite of this, Mother turned in and made a home for sister Peggy and the writer and in due course—heroic achievement for a bereaved Victorian lady—sent the writer to Radcliffe College, Cambridge, Massachusetts.

A new and wonderful world. This is IT. A professor's family takes her under their wing and introduces her to the world of Music—at top level. The world's finest symphonies are played on a parlor organ Sunday mornings; and a professor-father (with his Heavenly wife) expects each of their three daughters (Rosalie, Priscilla and Hildegarde), plus this wide-eyed waif from another state, to *think, express, react to life* in philosophical and psychological terms. Also we were expected to unload false gods, which we did with great zeal and thoroughness. Maine in the summer; Cambridge in the winter; and all along a rich affection given by this family and coupled with a zest for life in comfortable but not ornate material surroundings. Those were potent days.

College was rich too. Dormitory life with unpretentious and very human young girls. Singing Beethoven's 9th Symphony with the Harvard Glee Club and the Boston Symphony Orchestra. A few sprees with men friends such as Harvard Class Day. Everyone kind and friendly and a spirit of mental maturity and high adventure prevailing. Absorption of philosophy, history, and English literature, with a little science. These seemed a matter of course at the time, but furnished a background without which it would have been hard to understand the long long travail of Mankind up to now. In Spiritual, mental and material ways Man has indeed agonized to dispel his deep puzzlement as to his why, wherefrom and whither and as to how we are to resolve our life into what we Intuitively feel it is intended to be. Without this long-range view we cannot evaluate our present status, nor feel the compassion we should feel concerning his gigantic but incomplete efforts thus far.

We thought we had it made at college. The intellectual world was IT. Higher *Spiritual* Help we had none. They did not give It because they did not have It. Old emotional traditions were scorned and replaced by intellectual considerations. But the great, shining Mystic Truths, Which contain a purified and Universalized emotion plus a rational, *complete* intellectualism, were absent from our ken.

For instance, tho we studied Mankind's thirst for dominion and the very harsh story of his conquests in three dimensions, we were given very little understanding of his attendant yearning for Inner *self*-conquest. This *legitimate* passion is visible underneath his outer history if so be that a person, by Intuition, becomes aware of the transcendent *Spiritual*

Powers latent in all Individualized units of Be-ing. Without this Intuition, intellectualism becomes static; and the Universe appears as a mass of cold, purposeless defeatism. Without true, *scientific* Mysticism, intellectuals are in danger of ending their glorious contribution to human culture in a limbo of disappointment.

Similarly, on the other hand, without our present-day *intellectual* and *scientific* development, Mystics are in danger of becoming unconvincing in their unrealistic (pious) illusions.

In all human cultures tho, there are Sparks of illumined Vision. Mystics speak their piece tho seemingly to very small audiences. And as the centuries pass, these Sparks are articulated in more and more acceptable terms for the scientific mind. Take for instance James Russell Lowell's daring concept of the borning Self-Awareness latent in even the *Mineral* Life-Wave;

> "Whether we look or whether we listen
> We hear life murmur and see it glisten;
> Every clod feels a stir of might,
> An instinct within it that reaches and towers
> And groping blindly above it for light,
> Climbs to a soul in grass and flowers."*

Or Wordsworth's;

> "Our birth is but a sleep and a forgetting;
> The Soul that rises with us, our life's Star
>   Hath had elsewhere its setting
>   And cometh from afar!
>   Not in entire forgetfulness
>   Not in utter nakedness,
> But trailing clouds of glory do we come
>   From God Who is our Home."†

*From "The Vision of Sir Launfal"—by James Russell Lowell
†From "Ode on the Intimations of Immortality" by William Wordsworth

Sincere intellectualism such as we received at Radcliffe does indeed go a long step towards Mystic Revelation. The philosophic type of teaching in particular endeavors to work *upwards* from observed phenomena and comes close at times to acknowledging the Higher Principle. But even this noble attempt tends to shun phenomena which it cannot explain. And to us, the sum total of the philosophy of the ages leaned quite heavily on the defeatist side.

Does our traditional philosophy welcome the persistent "miracles" which dot the annals of history? On the contrary it tends to shelve them as Old Wives' Tales. Does Jesus Christ head the list of human philosophers as having mastered the art of observing *and controlling* the phenomena of Earth? On the contrary, Jesus Christ is conspicuously absent from most philosophy and psychology courses (or at least that was the writer's experience in the 1920's). And it would seem that His Guiding Principle—the Principle of Universal, *Causative*, Indwelling but Transcendent Spirit is not even suspected by most as a workable *scientific* Reality.

Webster says that Metaphysics is "the part of philosophy concerned with the ultimate causes—of things." If one had arrived at the "ultimate causes" would one not be *in control* of things? Assuredly one would be, as was Jesus—of gravity (walking on the water); of the ethers (producing loaves and fishes); of physical and psychological destructive forces (Healings); and finally of the deteriorated cells of His own body (in the Resurrection and Ascension). But we do not find this coveted control in the halls of learning in spite of their marvelous progress in investigating *secondary* causation in both scientific and philosophic channels.

True the study of secondary causation has given us mechanical aids which offer *a degree* of authority over the laws of physics and of psychology. But these methods as seen today are cumbersome, dangerous, fabulously expensive, and *incomplete*. A space-suit, for instance, is not a satisfying solution for the problem of adapting our organism to the

Inner dimensions. It is like the old error of building the Tower of Babel "to reach to Heaven." It was constructed from *without*; whereas the Kingdom of Heaven is *Within*. And it ended in confusion.

So we submit that the Mystic method of *Inner* Evolvement (Spiritual character-development) is better than over-emphasis on either mental or physical build-up from *outer* logic. And that it must be and shall be the last lap of the Path by which we recognize and harmonize with Ultimate Cause (Universal Spirit). Only by this harmonization, which is the natural result of illumined Self-Awareness, can we learn to control our destiny.

Our Spirit *projects* our body; and it is far easier for us to work from Within and change the projection (yes, we *can* change our bodies to conform with the perfect Archetype which Jesus manifested) than it is to invent space-suits to accommodate our present Earth-bound organism.

For this final step in our Self-Fulfillment we recognize intellectual and scientific development as an essential attribute *provided it* recognizes that "There cometh One mightier than I," Which is the *Spiritual* Faculty of Man. Jesus' final Demonstration was not only in His mind, but in His *body* (The Resurrection and the Ascension). And so must ours be also.

The Resurrection and Ascension Demonstrations of Jesus Christ are the ultimate proof of the Cosmic Authority which is ours when we penetrate the Realm of Ultimate Cause and harmonize our Individuality with our Parent-Source. "As the Father hath life in Himself; so hath He given to the Son to have life in *Him*self." The generic Son means each of us.

When I found some of the great Answers years later and began to *prove* them, I tried to share them with former associates in the halls of learning. They would have none of it. They were not interested, period. However, such a gigantic scientific mind as that of Albert Einstein believed devoutly in God; and most of our astronauts are very reverent people. The proud grandfather of a space-genius once told me "You have to get out into outer space to realize these Mystic Truths." Ralph Waldo Emerson was both philosopher and Mystic; and many doctors and highly trained intellects acknowledge the Higher Principle in a very rational way. So we gladly believe that this is the Age when all types of mind can meet at the top of the hill and learn from each other *provided* that we all admit that we do not know everything *yet*. This admission is the essence of the quality of *humility*, which is a first requirement for advancement at any level of our Evolvement.

Physical science is our doubting Thomas, to whom the Lord said "Blessed are they who have *not* seen and yet have believed."

Farewell then to this rich chapter of my progress—the intellectual stage. Many many thanks to the faithful parents who, by severe sacrifice, made it possible for me to drink deeply of the river of Man's intellectual and scientific achievements. These contain without doubt more than a drop of the still higher rivers of his Metaphysical Fulfillment. Many thanks too to Radcliffe with her dedicated leaders and teachers who give generously of the very best of Man's inherited treasure. One of Radcliffe's particularly inspired principles is that they realize they can give only a drop of the accumulated knowledge of the ages. This they give in such a way that it can impregnate the Intuitive student with the desire and the ability to use her mind for the final upward Reach which develops the Mystic Individuality (or Sonship Principle). So by implication they do recall John-the-Baptist who pointed his followers to the "One mightier than I." Thank you, Radcliffe. Thank you forever.

And many thanks too to my generous adopted family who gave Love and Appreciation and stimulated my enquiring Spirit.

New York City as seen from the East Side slums! My Aunt headed a Settlement House on East 60th Street and she and her sister most tenderly chaperoned my first plunge into the Great Unsheltered World. A job for me on Wall Street, which affected me about as a barrel of sawdust would affect a fish. I kept that job (executive work in a Trust Company) for 10 years and it furnished just the discipline I needed. Even tho one is an intellectual, reaching towards Something which one will later term Metaphysics, one must positively fight and win the battle to connect on intimate and creditable terms with Humanity as a whole in practical, material ways. This training is invaluable. It develops self-confidence, human understanding, and down-to-earthness. One must speak the language if one is to hold one's job; and when the Great Depression came along one must hold one's job or else.

Marriage! Life in the beautiful suburb of Scarsdale, New York. Commuting, tennis, and final emergence from the black jaws of the Depression. Beginnings of interest in social-economic issues, as the vibrant voice of Franklin Roosevelt proclaimed "There is nothing to fear but fear." This of course was a great *Metaphysical* pronouncement.

California beckoned. Friend husband would have none of it. He had turned ultra-conservative. No babies. He did not want any. Too risky in this questionable world. No Creative ambitions loomed on the horizon for us—just routine money-making. We parted friends, tho with great agony of Spirit; for our young-love chapter had been a beautiful one.

We had discovered the lectures of Emmet Fox and a great Light had come into my life. But to friend husband his old battle-scarred world was preferable. We no longer communicated. That choice of parting was the greatest choice we could have made. One cannot put new wine in old bottles.

California! In a two-seater, second-hand Ford. With my big dog Dusty. Tho the heart-pain was excruciating—leaving friend husband and our hard-won, beautiful home—yet we both knew that we could not have done otherwise. California meant Spiritual freedom to me; and it has proved so.

Not knowing a soul west of the Mississippi, I told people "Oh yes, I have friends in California—7 million of them."

And so it turned out. Never have I received anything but kindness, understanding, and a boost upwards. For most Californians believe in that Something Beyond. They are looking for It too; and they recognized their Spiritual sister in a moment. However, if that Something Beyond had not had me in Its keeping, I should have disappeared conclusively into one of the deep chasms which I blithely skirted in my Faith-filled Innocence.

Picking berries that first summer of the war. A sleeping bag in a government tent with Dusty keeping watch—all her primitive faculties on the alert. 25¢ a pail for berries and a lot of experience of life at rock-bottom level!

Eventual return to civilization and marriage to a Metaphysician. "The thing which will keep us together" said Charles, "Is that we both follow the Father." HMMMMM! Something wrong with that statement. Within a year we were older and wiser people. A tail to Charles' kite? Not for this had I sacrificed my Scarsdale idyll and plunged into the Unknown in a two-seater Ford. From that day on I knew I must go it alone. What was in me to give to the world I must give on my own terms. But Charles had shown me a new world—the Metaphysical world. What I had learned mentally with Emmet Fox in New York, I now saw in operation.

30,000 miles we travelled in the two-seater Ford. I was introduced to New Thought centers and people from Oregon to Florida. Another link in my education,—and I have a notion that I was another link in Charles' experience.

Los Angeles—City of the Angels! I had determined since Wall Street to work with *people*, not *property*. Nurses' aides are always in demand and they have a chance to contact people in a very wonderful way. Sick people are up against the deep issues of life, and they respond to the good-will of a person who believes in Life, in the rationality of this Earth-Plan, and who considers people—*all* people—Sons and Daughters of the Most High. So nurses' aiding furnished a means of sustenance when needed, and was an outlet for such Spiritual Power as I then possessed.

Edwyn Melby, chiropractor! Edwyn believes that the body can be rejuvenated. He generously thrusts this life-saving belief at anyone who will listen. I gave colonics for him in exchange for his moral and physical boost. Soon I was living with nutritionists and had become Vegetarian to the core. Under Edwyn's gentle, but inexorable guidance, I took 8 long fasts—one every year. They changed my thought-grooves, eliminating old hang-overs from the past; and doing the same for the body. A new world dawns and the body-bogey is beginning to be exorcised. (Fasts are wonderful but cannot be undertaken without competent professional advice.)

Nutrition, however, is not the whole answer. After a time I tired of the endless chopping of health salad, discussion of this or that vitamin, this or that combination of foods etc which went on in Nellie's kitchen. Nellie took in roomers—mostly of the Metaphysical persuasion. But to my mind they were "trying to get to Heaven on a diet" which, as Emmet Fox once remarked, is an impossibility.

My ethic regarding food is simple. I don't like death. Never have. Even a dead rabbit gives me a negative shock. "They shall not hurt nor destroy in all my Holy Mountain; for the Earth shall be filled with the knowledge of the Lord as the waters cover the sea." Why then should I *eat* dead animals? I don't. And that's it. I feel much better than before and the Inner Wisdom shows me what to eat and what not to eat. Since the fasts, my body usually wants what it should have—as nearly as possible taken in its natural state, not hepped up to appeal to jaded palates. No dead foods. No stimulants. No pastry nor cake nor white sugar nor white flour (all of which are devitalized foods as a rule). And very little salt. But plenty of *live* foods which taste better and better as the system becomes unclogged from artificial deli-cacies. This system has served me well and joyfully for 32 years, thanks to Edwyn's loving and very excellent coaching.

(Some such counselling is necessary for the budding Vegetarian, as there are many wrong turnings which one can take.)

Good-bye Edwyn. Good-bye Nellie. I must go it alone again. But thank you. *Thank you* forever.

George enters the picture. At Nellie's I had sent out the World Prayer Call. Nellie and Edwyn and Cynthia had helped me greatly and it had won us Spiritual friends around the world. In a small apartment overlooking Los Angeles from a hill near Echo Park Lake I followed this work and started to write seriously. George helped; believing in the work and himself becoming a Vegetarian. "I have to if I'm going to keep up with you" said George.

Copious reading of *many* angles of New Age Metaphysics had become a habit with me, and now to the reading was added personal contact by mail with global leaders and illumined Individuals the world over. It was a rich chapter in my Ongoing.

Hemet Valley after retirement. A new chapter as the work deepened and now reached into 28 countries and 30 states of the Union. Mail was an education in itself. The response to the books was gratifying in Spiritual terms, and very soul-warming. My blessed Mother had sometimes sent me financial help even tho she did not go along with my Spiritual views. Now she passed, and left me the wherewithal to start publishing.

Printing of books! Mail from around the world. 50,000 of the Prayer cards sent out to Individuals and groups around the world who redistributed them. Greater Peace than ever before and a sense of Right-ness and Advancement. And then—you will see from the next chapter what happened then.

CHAPTER 22

Zero Hour

A fall from the faithful blue bicycle. Vertebrae dislodged in the neck plus other injuries.

Found self in a Convalescent Hospital with a grim prognosis. Could not walk; could not eat; could not think; and was speedily on my way to Higher Ground according to medical authorities.

Three illumined friends refused to accept this verdict. In the demolition of my apartment Annea salvaged the lifeline of the world-work, my mailing list of 300 Spiritual names. She also informed hospital authorities that God could and would raise me up if so be that He wished me to do more work on Earth. Jack and Venice took over business matters, laboring long and lovingly to conserve assets in spite of horrendous medical costs. These three and others also prayed mightily in their own Individual ways. Also Dr. Helen Sanders, now of Garden Valley, Idaho, had given me preventive therapy for many years under her own original drugless method. This therapy I consider the next best thing to pure Spiritual Treatment; and I have no doubt that she had built up my tissues and organs so that they were able to do much better than average in a crisis. Dr. Sanders specializes in Prevention. She calls her method Neuro-muscular Therapy.

(Also I feel that Vegetarianism is a great physical asset.)

This does not in the least detract from the "miracle" of my recovery. Dr. Sanders herself is a miracle, believing as she does that the body is made to *live*, not die; and treating as she does the most severe cases of body tragedies with outstanding success. After all, a miracle is only a human accomplishment over and above the level previously observed by the recorders of the world's statistics. The files of the category enthusiasts do not contain such an occurrence? Then it did not occur in the average mind. But it *has* occurred—all down the ages, stemming from a Principle higher than Mankind as a whole has yet perceived. Presently tho, the proof of this is becoming overwhelming so that the miracle of today will become the commonplace of tomorrow in a better and happier world.

We do not wish to belittle the keepers of the world's statistics. It is necessary for the sake of Order that Man's experiences should be stashed away in categorical fashion. We are rich in being able to consult the shelves of our myriad reference rooms. Otherwise the vaulting imaginations of both competent and incompetent reporters would create utter confusion. So both liberal and conservative minds are necessary to offset each other as we progress haltingly upwards.

But sometimes we opine that some conservatives overstate their case a trifle as doubtless do some liberals also.

It would seem that body abberrations may stem from various levels. Some people today are accomplishing remarkable healings by regimes of natural physical measures such as diet, sun-bathing, exercises etc. Some work wonders on the psychic level by expelling obsessing entities or by dissolving their milder counterparts—dominations. And some are helped by mental-emotional means such as psychiatry. So it seems clear that some body ailments are caused by errors on the physical level, some by errors on the emotional or psychic levels, and some by errors on the mental level. All of these of course are intertwined.

Jesus treated some conditions differently from others. Sometimes He said "What do you wish me to do?" This aligned the patient's *emotions* into a clear, purposeful channel. Sometimes He said "Do you *believe* that I can do this?" This challenged the patient's *mental* orentation. With obsessions He addressed the invading entity rather than the patient. "Come out of him." And they did.

So we must be sure that our psychic channels are clear (no interference by invading entities); that our emotions are upward aligned (no confusion in our desires); and that our minds are admitting (believing) the Higher Power of Universal Spirit. In this way we allow the very Universal Christ to speak thru all our Be-ing "I will. Be thou whole." It will be so, provided we have asked "in Faith, *believing*."

Prayer does not work? Then why did Annea, one fine day, find me "sitting up and *smiling*" whereas I had been for some time in a condition where one friend thought I had already passed? Most fortunately, enough work had been done in my subconscious so that I had been able to receive the generous Help which was directed my way.

So I have had the joy of experiencing a slow return to Earth-life (a Resurrection), watching the body increasingly respond to the knowledge of Continuous Conscious Life which is our Birthright. Some believe, tentatively, that I actually died and returned; and whether this is so or not, I know that there was a mighty Clearance on the lower layers of my subconscious. Elemental racial fears must have been dissolved; for life is sweeter, quieter and far more understandable than before. I no longer think in terms of hurry. We are not rushing to forestall inevitable dissolution. We make our own conditions timewise and otherwise; and when fully illumined we can operate on Earth as long as we need to for *God*-Purposes. *We* project our bodies and our circumstances according to the beliefs which we have accepted in past and present lives. What do we believe? A jumble of confused and very egocentric conclusions for the most part. Consequently the crystallization of these in our bodies frustrates the Divine Self which we *are* so that in about fourscore years we are obliged to scrap our vehicles, return to our Parent-Source (Universal Spirit) and start again on a higher spiral. We go thru many Resurrections on our way up the Evolutionary ladder. But we are now in line for that final one after which death and darkness shall be no more.

Death is wonderful. It relieves us from the great tension of our mistakes. But it will not be necessary when we understand ourselves. We can accomplish this Clearance by "dying daily" as Paul said. By this we assume he meant the Sacrament of Spiritual Communion. As we have said, this Sacrament is our Opportunity to discard the outworn beliefs and emotions which have crystallized our Spirit into immobility.

This jumble of outworn beliefs and emotions is in our subconscious where we cannot easily get at it? That is what we are on Earth for. The all-wise Cosmic Law throws it up to us in binding situations of which body ailments are only one type. In Divine Order we shall always meet the people and circumstances which outpicture unsolved knots in our subconscious. Most of these we have tried to deal with in previous lives and have not made the grade. Therefore they appear again in more severe form and will appear periodically in this or future lives until we positively cease trying to gild over the surface and meet them face to face. As we have said, Forgiveness—both ways—is the solution to karmic tie-ups. Forgiveness is not completed until we are in harmony with our God, our selves, and the six-and-a-half billion brothers and sisters of our own Life-Wave. We come to grips with these karmic tie-ups on the physical level by service to the Race; on the psychological level by Understanding and Love; and on the Spiritual level by that Mystic Stream which the Lord said would flow out of our "belly" when we understand and embody the Word of Truth.

Giving out from the head is not enough. When that wonderful brain is illumined, we can indeed give out much intellectually. But to emulate that total Outpouring by which Jesus healed Himself and the Race, the Divine Inflow (the Odic Stream) must be consciously channelled from the brain to the solar plexus so that It can Regenerate the whole body and indeed flow out to the Cosmos from the "belly." "Out of his belly shall flow rivers of living water." The belly also probably includes that lowest situated of the twelve Faculties

of Man—the Generative Center, symbolized in the Bible by
Judas Iscariot. Judas is the last of our twelve Faculties to be
Regenerated. When redeemed, the Generative Center becomes the Resurrection Center. It then functions *upwards*,
giving Life to the whole body instead of *drawing from* it as
it did when it functioned downwards and was used illegiti-
mately (for excess sense-satisfaction).

Yes, the Resurrection is scientific and actual, not only
theoretical and imaginative. We go thru many partial Resurrections on our way to Glory. Can we now make It final and
complete?

CHAPTER 23

Zero Plus One

Never shall I believe that human nature is otherwise than fundamentally Good. The Medical profession, represented by nurses, aides, staff, volunteer helpers, cooks and even doctors, *rejoiced* when their worst predictions were reversed. They labor day and night in a seemingly futile attempt to deprive an inexorable force called "death" of its prey. They were delighted to see him frustrated for once; which means to me that even the self-styled materialist knows and loves the Truth of Life-everlasting for *all*. Life is all-victorious and will presently prove Itself, conclusively, in three dimensions for *everyone*.

Three years later, having graduated to the Retirement Home at Meadowbrook, Hemet, California, I would cross the compound and return to my old battle-ground—their Convalescent Hospital. Here I would sing hymns for the workers who clamored for this daily uplift. People whom I did not even remember would take time out to greet me. "What a *miracle* to see you walking down the hall!" What a miracle indeed! And what a joy!

As soon as I had collected my faculties after the long blank-out of desperate illness, I had a talk with the doctor. He was rather young and, by the Grace of God, not too arbitrary. He had put me thru innumerable tests but still did not feel that he knew it all. He was suggesting yet one more test. This time I rebelled.

"Doctor" I said "I don't want any more tests, biopsies, or whatever. If I have to go down the hill I want to go as comfortably as possible and I certainly don't want to *prolong* it."

126

"It's up to you" said the doctor. Bless him forever for that. "Think it over" he said kindly.

"I *have* thought it over" I said. I hadn't exactly *thought* about it. I just *knew*.

The head nurse, who witnessed this conversation, saw the Spiritual Factor at work in this situation. In fact she had contributed largely to this Factor, "He showed himself a great man" was her verdict for the doctor. And with this I heartily agree. He too recognized a Factor higher than materia medica.

So Elizabeth (the head nurse) and I are friends forevermore. As I recovered, she and I joined forces to do what we could Spiritually to further the New Age at Meadowbrook. And this being a remarkably idealistic group, we met with considerable success.

As soon as possible I talked the doctor (and/or Elizabeth) out of the heavy drugging which I was under. Perhaps drugs were advantageous during the emergency as they did seem to relieve the body and mind of excessive tensions. But if this release is bought at the cost of deadening the Higher Faculties (and it seems to me that this is exactly what it does), I believe a person makes a very great mistake in continuing drugs of *any* kind over a long period. Later still I left off pills of all kinds (even vitamins); and returned to my happy Vegetarian state. Attempts to improve on Mother Nature seem to me possibly valuable as a temporary measure but unnatural and often disastrous as a Way of life.

My three years at Meadowbrook were—for the most part—a ball. Even at the Retirement Home there was a certain recognition that a Higher Power was accomplishing my recovery. As in the whole world today a certain recognition is beginning to dawn. Many in the world are graduating from the freshman state where "They don't know; but they don't know that they don't know" and coming to the sophomore category where "They don't know; but they *know* that they don't know." Some again are juniors. "They know but they don't know that they know." And a few are tentatively but

128

surely approaching the senior stage where they grandly "know and they *know* that they know."

May all arrive there fast. But not *too* fast. To get our signals garbled and act like a senior when we really have considerable freshman work yet to do is disastrous—both for the person himself and for those who are forced to deal with him in close association. On the other hand there are those who *should* be seniors but who do not wish to take the responsibility of that status. They behave like underclassmen and so deprive the Race of much aid and comfort which it is entitled to and which it desperately needs.

At all events, young, old and middle-aged at Meadowbrook were in general quite receptive to elementary Principles of the Resurrection when presented to them not in abstract, but in flesh and blood terms. The considerate and highminded attitude of the workers and staff at Meadowbrook also shows a knowledge of the Higher Principles.

All Healing is Spiritual. So there is really no hard and fast line between the Spiritual and the "material" beliefs.

Take for instance the prominent surgeon who was informed one day that a little boy had had his arm torn off in an accident. The surgeon immediately retired to prepare himself for major action. He brushed up on the technical aspects of his challenge—the anatomy of the upper arm. And he gathered his forces to say "No" to impending disaster in the Name of the All-Life (Wholeness) to which surgeons are dedicated.

When the little boy arrived on a stretcher with his arm following in an ice-basket, the surgeon was ready. He and his assistant took the challenge in Divine Order. Bones, muscles, blood-vessels, nerves, tissues and skin—they took turns spelling each other off in a 7-hour ordeal. When the flush of life flowed thru the Resurrected arm, they knew the Joy of the Lord.

This surgeon did not take time out to say "Man is born to suffer so I will just sew up the mutilated shoulder." He did not see a severed arm. He saw a boy who would soon be a man and who was created perfect and could remain so. All of these attitudes are accredited Metaphysical Principles.

Our surgeon was a Christian in spirit—whatever may have been his intellectual explanation of his Inner philosophy. Christians believe that God is Wholeness and that He-She created Man in His-Her own Image. *And* that when Man slips in his efforts to objectify that Image, there is perfect Forgiveness, or Restoration, in the Name of the One Perfect Source. Resurrection takes place (for ourself or for someone else) to the extent that we are able to *know* this thru all our subconscious Be-ing and to apply all our faculties to giving it out *completely.*

Did Jesus know the anatomy of the upper arm? We feel sure that He did, or that it was immediately available to Him from the Akashic Records if He needed it. But He did not need to manipulate mentally the lower details of His Healings any more than He needed forceps or ligatures. Speaking directly from First Cause He enlisted Nature's Creative Power, which as a rule worked instantaneously from the level of Universal Spirit downwards to the finished product on Earth.

Did He know what ailed Lazarus? Assuredly He did. But He did not have to delve into physical details since He knew the *Spiritual* causes which limited both Lazarus and those who in their ignorance were binding him with graveclothes (or in other words holding him in the death consciousness by their fears, grief and defeatism). "Loose him and let him go" said Jesus. And it was so.

We believe that Jesus wept at the grave, not because of this one death, which He knew He could reverse, but because of the pitiable condition of the Human Spirit which stands, helpless and defeated, against the false claims of nether suggestions.

Jesus worked from First Cause downwards (outwards); so He did not need consciously to pile up anatomical details from exterior knowledge. He could and did on occasion use

such aids as mineral water. "Go bathe in the pool of Siloam."
But we remember that names to the Jewish people meant
Principles. So He was really referring His patient to certain
Spiritual Truths. Using His own saliva with the Earth to
make clay was also an object lesson, the abstract meaning
of which was undoubtedly known to His students and probably to most of the Jewish people.

Jesus worked *always* with and from Universal Spirit
(Principle) and *never* gave authority to an inert, soul-less
factor which Mrs. Eddy has well christened "The *supposi-
tional* opposite of God."

CHAPTER 24

Rainbows at Last

Having surrendered the idea of being able to return to world work, I lived for three years at Meadowbrook in a mental blank. Perhaps this was necessary as a rest from the feeling of responsibility. Spiritual service was possible to a small extent by the playing and singing of hymns, which was an acceptable form of Inspiration to many. It seems to me that some of the old hymns go further than most sermons in presenting Higher Truths. Strange that the Race can accept in poetry and song much deeper principles than they will accept in prose!

What was my astonishment then, after 3 years of mental inertia, to have Jack inform me that 43 boxes of my books were reposing gently under the tables in his print shop! It seemed unbelievable. I had resigned myself to the probability that they had been scrapped, since there had seemed no likelihood of my being able to do anything with them. Jack is a very unpretentious person; but one could feel his sense of deep satisfaction at having put in such a potent strike for what he considered a worthwhile cause. He had kept the Faith when there had seemed no rational basis for It. It had not been easy; and neither had the financial situation been easy. With a hailstorm of medical bills flying at them, Jack and Venice had managed to preserve my living principal so that they now presented me with, not only the means of subsistence, but enough to spare so that the world work could be resumed! Also Annea and Evelyn had carried, stored, and now returned to me my clothes and other gadgets for comfortable living!

What joy! What deep and abiding joy—to know that the

Divine Plan had restored me to Its Service! And thru such loving channels as these deeply Spiritual but practical-minded friends! When Annea brought my Resurrection picture (taken from the one at Forest Lawn), which she had salvaged from the old apartment, we were in business again—world-wide.

The picture hangs in this little bachelor apartment. It sets the keynote for the work which is again being carried abroad. More so than before in fact; for the books have found channels thru two excellent Metaphysical distributors—De Vorss & Co, of Marina del Rey, California, and Mr. Harold Ingraham, of Ashland Oregon.

I can only testify that the Christian pattern set by Jesus does include our descent into the depths of Human experience. How else could we know these depths consciously—know them and so relate emotionally to *all* other Humans, who also are experiencing the same in various and sundry ways?

Each descent assures a Return, tho perhaps in a different body, depending on the condition of our subconscious. Until that last final descent when we shall consciously know *all* Human experience and be able to deal with it for Good instead of for defeat.

Where do we go from here? Both the nose and the feet point *forward*; so where can we go but ahead? Some of course try to go backwards, or sidewise, or in circles, or in several directions at once, or to stand still. But this does not work very well. The whole sweep of the Cosmos is *forward* so it is much more pleasurable for ourselves and for our neighbors if we go forward at all costs, using the momentum of all the Higher Beings which The Lord brought to Earth and planted in our Consciousness.

Epilogue

It is said that there was a lady in Hiroshima who not only *survived* the atom bomb, but came out *rejuvenated*.

We do not vouch for this; but we certainly do accept the Principle which she is said to have enunciated. There are two *Rays* in every happening, was her philosophy. One is Life-Giving and the other is *de*structive. We choose which Ray we will tune in on.

Amen to that. And is not that Power of Choice the very essence of our Christ Identity as soon as we understand It and choose to choose aright?

In this century we are faced with a moral Hiroshima. How many of us can and will keep our stature and tune in on the *Life-Giving* Ray—that is, accept Life's great Gift *in us* and give It out *fully* to others? "As the Father hath Life in Himself; so hath He given to the Son to have Life in *Him*self." We are the Son; "*All* of you are Sons and Daughters of the Most High." Also "You are the Light of the world." "You are the salt of the Earth; but if the salt has lost its savor, wherewith shall it be salted?"

We know that there are many in various fields of endeavor who already realize this. And since we are Fishers of men, each Victory of ours serves as a magnet to draw others who are teetering on the brink of chaos.

It is from Jesus that we have the last Word on the subject of the Resurrection. "He who would save his life shall lose it; but whoso shall lose his life for my sake and the Gospel's shall save it unto Life Eternal." And "If a man keep my saying he shall never see death but is passed from death unto Life."

As He was, so can we be *if we try*.